C0046 58223

D1621188

GREAT SCOTTISH
SPEECHES

GREAT SCOTTISH SPEECHES

INTRODUCED AND EDITED BY DAVID TORRANCE

ટ**

WITH A FOREWORD BY ALEX SALMOND

Luath Press Limited

EDINBURGH

www.luath.co.uk

First published 2011

ISBN: 978 1906817 97 8

The paper used in this book is sourced from renewable forestry

MIX
Paper from
responsible sources
FSC® C018575

and is FSC credited material.

Printed and bound by
MPG Books Ltd., Cornwall

Typeset in 10.5 point Gill and 10.5 point Quadraat
by 3btype.com

Contents

*To robbery, slaughter, plunder, they give the lying name of empire;
they make a solitude and call it peace.*

*There is Christ Jesus... whose subject James the Sixth is,
and of whose kingdom he is not a king, nor a lord,
nor a head, but a member.*

*Life's but a walking shadow, a poor player that struts
and frets his hour upon the stage.*

*I go from a corruptible to an incorruptible crown;
where no disturbance can be, no disturbance in the world.*

*For none comes into the world with a saddle upon his back,
neither any booted and spurred to ride him.*

*None can destroy Scotland, save Scotland itself;
hold your Hands from the Pen, you are secure.*

I was brought up in true, loyal, and anti-revolution principles.

The History of the World... is the Biography of Great Men.

*We quit a vitiated Establishment –
but we shall rejoice to return to a poorer one.*

Foreword by Alex Salmond

Scots have always loved a good argument. We have a strong history and tradition of debate.

Indeed, a great compliment – and often challenge – to a fellow countryman or woman is to say that they have 'a guid Scots tongue' in their heid, and an obligation to make their voice heard.

So what some may describe as a national tendency to be disputatious, I prefer to think of as a commitment to speak up for what we think is right, to join in the discourse, and ultimately let the people decide.

And that is another aspect of our national character, the 'democratic intellect' – the strong belief that knowledge should be available to all, and that every citizen has the right to express their view without fear or favour, regardless of rank or station.

In Scotland, we have a shared and passionate commitment to the political and constitutional process as the determinant of change – which means that the force of argument decides what happens.

Therefore, as this book narrates, Scotland has always placed the highest value on the merits of a case – and its ability not just to persuade, but also inspire people to join a common cause.

And as this book also testifies, it is a tradition of our national story which reaches from the earliest times to the present day – and extends across the spectrum of political, religious, philosophical and scientific thought.

Throughout our history, we have had many different forums for national debate, as circumstances changed. Before our parliament was reconvened in 1999 after an adjournment of nearly 300 years, Scotland was nonetheless alive with passionate discourse on all sides and in many places – not least in the letters columns of our national newspapers!

It is an important part of our national life, and one that I hope this book helps foster. Public speaking can instil great self-confidence among young people, and we are blessed as a nation with so many talented young Scots with so much to offer – and with a guid Scots tongue in their heid.

As Scotland embarks on a new process of discussion and debate about our constitutional future, it is timely to celebrate the different voices and strands of opinion which have taken the nation to our present place – and to encourage new voices for our future progress.

Let the discourse begin!

The Rt Hon Alex Salmond MSP, First Minister of Scotland

Preface by Prof David Purdie

PSYCHOLOGISTS TELL US that neither the death of a parent nor the birth of a child, nor the beginning or ending of a partnership or love affair, is as terrifying to the generality of mankind than the looming requirement to give a public address. It need not be so. Great orators are few, but competence is within the reach of most people given adherence to the basics; especially the basic ability to get up, speak up and then shut up and sit down within the attention span of the audience.

In public speaking there are many rules and regulations but one – and only one – Golden Rule: Leave them wanting *more*. The finest compliment for an orator is to be told, collectively by ovation and individually by hearers, that they could have done with ten more minutes of that. So what makes a good speech? The question was first addressed by the greatest polymath of classical Athens, the Edinburgh of the South. Aristotle's great Treatise, *The Art of Rhetoric*, set out ground rules which are as valid today as when he formulated them two and a half millennia ago.

A speech must do three things: It must educate; it must entertain and finally it must *move* the audience. Persuasive speaking requires another triad: the speaker must be seen to be a master of the subject; the emotional content must fit that of the audience – and the speech must flow seamlessly from a gripping start to a logical middle and to a valid conclusion.

Throughout the address, a really good speaker will engage with the audience through eye contact and gesture, having first prepared for the occasion by following the famous five steps. These were set out by Marcus Cicero, Rome's greatest orator and writer on the subject: decide what to say; decide in what order to say it; decide the style of delivery; *memorise* it – and then deliver it. One other talent not possessed by all, but a huge asset if present, is the decoration of a speech with humorous anecdote and story. Scottish audiences particularly enjoy that magic mixture of education and entertainment when served up and garnished with the sauce of wit and analogy. All these ingredients you will find here in David Torrance's deft selection.

The English and Scots languages are the most powerful weapons that can be placed at your command. But language, like any other weapon system, requires cleaning and oiling and repeated testing to be sure of accuracy in the field, or in this case, on the platform. Misdirected, it can cause serious injury, but when mastered it can cause pleasure almost without limit.

The very first orator in European literature was Odysseus, King of Ithaca. Homer tells us in the *Iliad* that he was not a massive physical presence:

But, when let that voice go from his chest,
And his words came drifting down like winter's snows
Then no living man could stand against Odysseus.

In other words, he left them wanting *more*....

Prof David Purdie MD FRCP Edin. FSA Scot.

Introduction

THIS BOOK STARTED – unusually – as a status update on the social
networking website Facebook. I posted the following on 15 November 2010:

**David Torrance is on the hunt for Great Scottish Speeches (for a possible
book pitch). Any ideas? The only criteria is that the oratory was delivered by a
Scot, or in Scotland by anyone else...**

Despite this rather vague invitation, within a few days more than 60 people
had left comments, suggesting possible speeches and, in a few cases, simply
remarking how stimulating the discussion was. Neil Mackinnon, for example,
said it was 'possibly the longest and most interesting Facebook status update
comments list' he had seen. Heartened, I collected these together, added some of
my own, and took the idea to Gavin MacDougall at Luath Press, who
enthusiastically took it on board. Enthusiasm from a publisher is a rare and
therefore agreeable phenomenon!

Gavin was aware, as was I, of Richard Aldous's excellent collection of
Great Irish Speeches[1], which had been a bestseller in, naturally enough, Dublin
bookshops in the Christmas of 2007. I was already thinking of editing a Scottish
equivalent when I ordered a copy of Aldous's book online, but seeing it
confirmed in my mind that if Ireland's turbulent history could justify a book of
speeches, then so could Scotland's (admittedly less turbulent) past. As Aldous
told me by email, his book attracted a lot of media attention, 'primarily because
it allowed everyone to turn it into a parlour game – what's your favourite,
what else should have been in/out, which person should have been in/out, etc'.
I hoped mine would do the same, just as it had on Facebook.

Next came the criteria. Broken down, this fell into three parts. First, a speech
had to be 'Scottish', which I took to mean – as per my original Facebook posting
– speeches made by anyone (Scots and non-Scots) in Scotland or speeches made
by Scots anywhere else in the world. (I'll spare the reader a tortuous treatise on
what precisely constitutes a 'Scot'.) Next, and this may sound foolish, anything
worthy of inclusion had to be classifiably a 'speech'. In other words any piece of
oratory that sources confirmed had been delivered by its author, and of any
length from a paragraph up to several pages long (although for reasons of
brevity, most of the speeches in this collection have been edited down – I hope
sympathetically – to no more than four pages). Some did not qualify on this
basis. Several people suggested Jenny Geddes' interjection at St Giles' Cathedral
in 1637, but as it amounted to no more than a cry – 'Deil colic the wame o' ye,
fause thief; daur ye say Mass in my lug?'[2] – I had to leave it out, however
significant it was historically.

Finally, each speech had to be 'great'. Primarily, this came down to content;
a truly great speech needs to *say* something, make an argument with coherence

and brevity. It also needs to be well delivered, although in many cases content is more important than theatrical flourish; Sir David Maxwell Fyfe was not renowned as a great orator, but his speech at the signing of the European Convention on Human Rights in Rome was arguably historically important, and therefore 'great'. A great speech also requires a contemporary context that heightened its delivery to more than just words on a page: a simple, memorable idea that somehow defined the moment. Great oratory, in short, needs to be authentic.

As I gathered material, I became more flexible. It seemed a shame, for example, to exclude fictional oratory, so my criteria was relaxed to allow room for speeches from the pens of William Shakespeare, Muriel Spark and, more contemporaneously, Irvine Welsh. A speech is a speech, be it fictional or real, imagined or intended. Few if any of those in this collection would not have been considered 'speeches' at the moment of their delivery.

Which speeches have made it to the final cut – and I gathered enough material for around 100 – is, of course, highly subjective, although I have striven for political balance, given that most speeches are political in nature. Thus there is, I hope, a good spread of rhetoric (and I don't mean that in a pejorative sense) from Left and Right, Nationalist and Unionist. Some readers will inevitably start foaming at the mouth when they reach Margaret Thatcher's 1988 'Sermon on the Mound', but whether a speech is great or not does not come down to whether we like its speaker's politics. I hope that even the Iron Lady's most fervent critics could not deny the historical significance of her – after all sincere – oratory.

The process of tracking down the full texts of possible speeches was challenging, fun, time consuming and occasionally frustrating. With the exception of those delivered in the last few years (in which case the internet furnished me with the full text following a quick search), speeches, even contemporary ones, can be remarkably elusive. There are no Scottish suffragettes in this collection, for example, for although they gave hundreds of speeches at rallies across the country, contemporary newspaper coverage was paltry and subsequent scholarship incomplete.

Indeed, while I am on the subject of women, lest anyone consider me misogynistic, I *am* conscious that they are under-represented in this collection. I can only plead that the business of oratory is almost an entirely male category. Indeed, when *The Guardian* published a collection of great 20th-century speeches back in 2007, it obviously struggled to find female examples. The obvious explanation for this is that it was politicians who generally made speeches and, generally speaking, until recently Scottish politics was dominated by men.

Nevertheless, some have made their way into this collection, including the early female MP Frances Horsbrugh, the fictional Miss Jean Brodie and the robustly non-fictional Margaret Thatcher. As I have already mentioned, I searched in vein for extant speeches by Scottish campaigners for women's suffrage, and was also frustrated in my hunt for oratory by early female political activists such as Helen Crauford, who made numerous speeches during the rent strike of 1917. Unfortunately, no one thought to preserve them.

This problem extended even to better-known, and more recent, speeches by men. Harry Reid urged me to include the educationalist RF Mackenzie's plea for genuinely comprehensive education in 1974, observing that 'surely' someone had recorded his whole speech. Alas, they had not, and neither contemporary newspaper reports nor the Aberdeen Council archives gave me anything more than a few paragraphs. Even so, I pieced together what I could (including Reid's contemporary *Scotsman* reports) and it is included within these pages.

Other fields – for example the sporting fraternity – simply have not made many significant speeches. I tried hard to include some footballers, rugby coaches, even golfers. But while I located plenty memorable quotes, there was simply no extended oratory. Likewise with writers, poets and artists. If they had spoken at all, it was on a political matter, and political speeches rather dominated in any case. Jim Telfer's 1997 'Everest' speech was an honourable, and very worthy, exception.

If I am making my task sound impossible, I do not intend to, for other speeches were remarkably easy to track down. Anything Parliamentary, for example, could be traced via the excellent http://hansard.millbanksystems.com website, which contains – in digital form – almost everything uttered in the House of Commons over the last couple of centuries. Similarly, modern orators tended to be modest enough to post transcripts of recent triumphs on their personal websites, for example www.georgegalloway.info. Indeed, Gorgeous George's 2005 Washington performance is a fine example of a defensive or valedictory speech, echoing those made by others from the gallows, such as Lord Balmerino in 1746 and John Maclean in 1918. The difference, of course, is that today's speakers – having vindicated themselves – tend not to be hanged.

Several interesting things occurred to me as I researched this book, such as the impact of certain speeches on public opinion. We may think that the art of oratory no longer has any tangible effect beyond the political fraternity, but when you consider Sir Henry Campbell-Bannerman's brave stand against the 'barbarism' of the Boer War alongside Tommy Sheridan's speech against poindings and warrant sales almost a century later, it becomes clear that little, in some respects, has changed.

Indeed, talking of Sheridan highlights an important shift in the origins of significant oratory. 'The essential ingredient of a great speech, a sense of injustice or outrage,' observed the columnist Philip Collins in *The Times*, 'began to dwindle as life got less and less outrageous in the back half of the 20th century.' There is something in this, for as the austerity of the 1930s and '40s gave way to the post-war boom, there was simply less to make impassioned speeches about. The firebrand Tommy Sheridan, however, believed that even in the year 2000 there was still a lot to be angry about.

I noticed other consistent features, not least the need for great speeches to project a social or political vision, from the utopian plea for a 'Socialist Commonwealth' by Keir Hardie in 1901 to Thatcher's very different ideological perspective at the Church of Scotland in 1988. There were also cultural differences. Two Rectorial addresses, for example, are included in this collection, a platform for great oratory that has not existed in the other three parts of the United Kingdom (or indeed Ireland prior to 1922).

A quick note on the chronology. The earliest speech included here is that reputedly given by Calgacus in advance of the Battle of Mons Graupius in AD 83 or 84, from which a misquotation – 'they make a desert and call it peace' – would certainly be known to the Nationalist Alex Salmond, whose speech following the 2007 Holyrood election is the most recent.

What almost 20 centuries of Scottish oratory highlights, above all, is the changing expectations of the listening audience, another crucial – and much underrated – requirement for a great speech. From speeches intended to rouse troops going into battle, to the more recognisable political, legal and religious oratory of the 18th and 19th centuries, and finally to those of the 20th century, encompassing wars both hot and Cold, and the constitutional debate.

One can only imagine what those listening to Calgacus made of his speech (if indeed it ever took place), while a glance at verbatim newspaper reports of 19th-century speeches – complete with notes of 'Applause' and 'Laughter' at key moments – indicates that audiences used to listen to complex political arguments for hours. As the 20th century wore on, what audiences expected to hear changed, and great speechmakers had to adapt. There were fewer public meetings, and therefore fewer public speeches, but in an increasingly media-dominated landscape speakers found other means by which to reach their audiences, and speeches became much shorter as a result. There is, however, one striking constant: the remarkable and enduring power of the spoken word.

Finally, a book such as this inevitably creates debts, so thank you to everyone who suggested, or helped me track down, speeches, including Keith Aitken, Professor Richard Aldous (for advice when I first started this project), Gavin Bowd, Rebecca Bridgland, Jill Ann Brown, Jennifer Dempsie, Robbie Dinwoodie, Michael Donoghue, Stuart Drummond, Rose Dunsmuir, John Edward, Tom English, Bradley Farquhar, Colin Faulkner, Neil Freshwater, Professor Gregor Gall, Tom Gallagher, Sam Ghibaldan, Martyn Glass, Duncan Hamilton, Martin Hannan, Malcolm Harvey, Professor Christopher Harvie, Gerry Hassan, Bill Heaney, Andrew Henderson, Martin Hogg, Professor James Hunter, Peter Kearney, Jacq Kelly, Hugh Kerr, Ed Kozak, Lallands Peat Worrier, Graeme Littlejohn, Danny Livingston, Andrew Lownie, Andrew MacGregor, Iain Mackenzie, Neil Mackinnon, John MacLeod, Maxwell MacLeod, Carole McCallum, Patrick McFall, Iain McLean, Michael McManus, Sarah McMillan, Lynne McNeil, Professor James Mitchell, Brian Monteith, Kenny Morrison, David Mowbray, Andrea Mullaney, Timothy Neat, Dr Andrew Newby, Willis Pickard, Harry Reid, James MacDonald Reid, David Ritchie, James Robertson,

Jim Sillars, Graeme Stirling, Duncan Sutherland, DR Thorpe, Michael Torrance, the TUC Library, Alison Weir, Andy Wightman, Craig Williams, Mike Wilson, Donald Wintersgill, Canon Kenyon Wright, Jane Yeoman, Duncan Young and Eleanor Yule.

Please feel free to email me with suggestions for 'More' Great Scottish Speeches!

David Torrance
Edinburgh, July 2011
www.davidtorrance.com
Follow @davidtorrance on twitter

To robbery, slaughter, plunder,
      they give the lying name of empire;
they make a solitude and call it peace.

Calgacus
1st Century AD

SPEECH REPUTEDLY GIVEN IN ADVANCE OF THE
BATTLE OF MONS GRAUPIUS • NORTHERN SCOTLAND
AD 83 OR 84

According to Tacitus, the senator and historian of the Roman Empire, Calgacus was a chieftan in Caledonia who fought the Roman army of Gnaeus Julius Agricola at the Battle of Mons Graupius in northern Scotland. The only historical source, however, in which he appears is Tacitus's own *Agricola*, which describes him as 'the foremost in courage and the noblest in birth' of the Scottish chieftans. Tacitus also recounts the following short speech, the earliest in this collection, which he attributes to Calgacus.

Calgacus (sometimes styled Calgacos or Galgacus) is the earliest of only four named figures to feature in the history of Roman Scotland. Significantly, like the others, he bore a recognisably Celtic name, the equivalent of Calgaich, meaning 'swordsman' or 'swordbearer' – an element occasionally found in Irish Gaelic place names.

The speech, often misquoted as 'they make a desert and call it peace', describes the exploitation of Britain by Rome in order to rouse Calgacus's troops to fight. The site of this conflict, in which more than 30,000 native troops are supposed to have united in order to defend Caledonia (eastern Scotland, north of the Forth and Clyde), only to be routed by a numerically inferior Roman force, has yet to be conclusively identified, although it could have taken place between the rivers Don and Urie in Aberdeenshire.

The battle formed the decisive climax of Agricola's governorship (AD 77/8–83/4) and seems to have broken resistance to Rome in the north of Britain for almost two decades, inaugurating a military occupation of most of what is now lowland Scotland.

WHENEVER I CONSIDER the origin of this war and the necessities of our position, I have a sure confidence that this day, and this union of yours, will be the beginning of freedom to the whole of Britain. To all of us slavery is a thing unknown; there are no lands beyond us, and even the sea is not safe, menaced as we are by a Roman fleet. And thus in war and battle, in which the brave find glory, even the coward will find safety. Former contests, in which, with varying fortune, the Romans were resisted, still left in us a last hope of succour, inasmuch as being the most renowned nation of Britain, dwelling in the very heart of the country, and out of sight of the shores of the conquered, we could keep even our eyes unpolluted by the contagion of slavery. To us who dwell

I have sure confidence that this day,
and this union of yours, will be the beginning
of freedom to the whole of Britain

on the uttermost confines of the earth and of freedom, this remote sanctuary of Britain's glory has up to this time been a defence. Now, however, the furthest limits of Britain are thrown open, and the unknown always passes for the marvellous. But there are no tribes beyond us, nothing indeed but waves and rocks, and the yet more terrible Romans, from whose oppression escape is vainly sought by obedience and submission. Robbers of the world, having by their universal plunder exhausted the land, they rifle the deep. If the enemy be rich, they are rapacious; if he be poor, they lust for dominion; neither the east nor the west has been able to satisfy them. Alone among men they covet with equal eagerness poverty and riches. To robbery, slaughter, plunder, they give the lying name of empire; they make a solitude and call it peace.

In war and battle, in which the brave find glory,
even the coward will find safety.

There is Christ Jesus...
whose subject James the Sixth is,
and of whose kingdom he is not a king,
nor a lord, nor a head, but a member.

Andrew Melville
1545–1622

'INTERVIEW WITH THE KING' • FALKLAND PALACE • 1595

Andrew Melville was a university principal and theologian whose fame attracted scholars from across Europe to study at the Universities of St Andrews and Glasgow. He held the post of Rector at both of these seats of learning, but achieved added fame for campaigning to protect the Scottish Church from government interference. Although most accepted Melville was fighting to safeguard the constitutionally guaranteed rights of the Church, his critics believed him to be disrespectful of the monarch in the process.

In 1594 Melville was suspected by the King, apparently without foundation, of favouring the Earl of Bothwell, who had for a time supported Presbyterian objections to the King's recent arbitrary and illegal behaviour. In 1595, and again in 1596, Melville made his famous 'two kingdoms' speech on the separate nature of the ecclesiastical and civil jurisdictions to King James VI of Scotland (later to become King James I of England) at Falkland Palace. It worked, for as one historian recorded, during the delivery of this 'confounding speech his majesty's passion subsided'.

Andrew Melville was born near Montrose in Angus, and educated at the Universities of St Andrews and Paris. After travelling in Europe he returned to Scotland in 1574 and was appointed principal of Glasgow University, and thereafter principal of St Andrews. Melville was also moderator of the General Assembly of the Church of Scotland in 1578. Having annoyed the King, he was sent to the Tower of London for four years, and saw out the rest of his life in Sedan.

SIR, WE WILL ALWAYS humbly reverence your majesty in public; but since we have this occasion to be with your majesty in private, and since you are brought in extreme danger both of your life and crown, and along with you the country and the church of God are like to go to wreck, for not telling you the truth and giving you faithful counsel, we must discharge our duty, or else be traitors both to Christ and you. Therefore, Sir, at diverse times before I have told you, so now again I must tell you, there are two kings and two kingdoms in Scotland: there is King James, the head of this commonwealth, and there is Christ Jesus, the King of the church, whose subject James the Sixth is, and of whose kingdom he is not a king, nor a lord, nor a head, but a member. Sir, those whom Christ has called and commanded to watch over his church, have power and authority from him to govern his spiritual kingdom both jointly and severally; the which no Christian king or prince should control and discharge, but fortify and assist; otherwise they are not faithful subjects of Christ and members of his church. We will yield to you your place, and give you all due

You are brought in extreme danger both of your life and crown, and along with you the country and the Church of God are like to go to wreck.

obedience; but again I say, you are not the head of the church: you cannot give us that eternal life which we seek for even in this world, and you cannot deprive us of it. Permit us then freely to meet in the name of Christ, and to attend to the interests of that church of which you are the chief member. Sir, when you were in your swaddling-clothes, Jesus Christ reigned freely in this land in spite of all his enemies: his officers and ministers convened and assembled for the ruling and welfare of his church, which was ever for your welfare, defence, and preservation, when these same enemies were seeking your destruction and cutting off. Their assemblies since that time continually have been terrible to these enemies, and most steadable to you. And now, when there is more than extreme necessity for the continuance and discharge of that duty, will you (drawn to your own destruction by a devilish and most pernicious counsel) begin to hinder and dishearten Christ's servants and your most faithful subjects, quarrelling them for their convening and the care they have of their duty to Christ and you, when you should rather commend and countenance them, as the godly kings and emperors did? The wisdom of your counsel, which I call devilish, is this, that ye must be served by all sorts of men, to come to your purpose and grandeur, Jew and Gentile, Papist and Protestant: and because the Protestants and ministers of Scotland are over strong and control the kind, they must be weakened and brought low by stirring up a party against them, and, the king being equal and indifferent, both shall be fain to flee to him. But, Sir, if God's wisdom be the only true wisdom, this will prove mere and mad folly; his curse cannot but light upon it: in seeking both ye shall lose both; whereas, in cleaving uprightly to God, his true servants would be your sure friends, and he would compel the rest counterfeitly and lyingly to give over themselves and serve you.

Life's but a walking shadow, a poor player that struts and frets his hour upon the stage.

Macbeth

FICTIONAL

SOLILOQUY FROM THE PLAY MACBETH • 1611

The Macbeth of Shakespeare's play was largely drawn from Raphael Holinshed's *Chronicles*, published in 1577. Holinshed had been heavily influenced by the writings of Hector Boece, who asserted, without any authority, that Macbeth had been 'thane' of Glamis and Cawdor, a styling then picked up by Shakespeare.

The unspoken conflict in this speech – one of the playwright's great soliloquies – is that between free will and predestination, or in other words the King's inability to overcome his darker temptations. The appearance of a bloody dagger in the air unsettles Macbeth, who does not know if it is real or a figment of his guilty imagination as he contemplates killing Duncan.

William Shakespeare was born in Stratford in 1564 into a relatively prosperous family. Details of his life are sketchy, although it is known he married at 18 and thereafter spent most of his time in London writing and performing his plays. He died in 1616.

MACBETH

Is this a dagger which I see before me,
The handle toward my hand? Come, let me clutch thee.
I have thee not, and yet I see thee still.
Art thou not, fatal vision, sensible
To feeling as to sight? or art thou but
A dagger of the mind, a false creation,
Proceeding from the heat-oppressed brain?
I see thee yet, in form as palpable
As this which now I draw.
Thou marshall'st me the way that I was going;
And such an instrument I was to use.
Mine eyes are made the fools o' the other senses,
Or else worth all the rest; I see thee still,
And on thy blade and dudgeon gouts of blood,
Which was not so before. There's no such thing:
It is the bloody business which informs

Thus to mine eyes. Now o'er the one halfworld
Nature seems dead, and wicked dreams abuse
The curtain'd sleep; witchcraft celebrates
Pale Hecate's offerings, and wither'd murder,
Alarum'd by his sentinel, the wolf,
Whose howl's his watch, thus with his stealthy pace.
With Tarquin's ravishing strides, towards his design
Moves like a ghost. Thou sure and firm-set earth,
Hear not my steps, which way they walk, for fear
Thy very stones prate of my whereabout,
And take the present horror from the time,
Which now suits with it. Whiles I threat, he lives:
Words to the heat of deeds too cold breath gives.

> *Art thou but/ A dagger of the mind, a false creation/*
> *Proceeding from the heat-oppressed brain?*

MACBETH
Wherefore was that cry?

SEYTON
The queen, my lord, is dead.

MACBETH
She should have died hereafter;
There would have been a time for such a word.
To-morrow, and to-morrow, and to-morrow,
Creeps in this petty pace from day to day
To the last syllable of recorded time,
And all our yesterdays have lighted fools
The way to dusty death. Out, out, brief candle!
Life's but a walking shadow, a poor player
That struts and frets his hour upon the stage
And then is heard no more: it is a tale
Told by an idiot, full of sound and fury,
Signifying nothing.

I go from a corruptible to an incorruptible crown; where no disturbance can be, no disturbance in the world.

Charles I
1600–1649

SPEECH FROM THE SCAFFOLD • BANQUETING HOUSE • LONDON

30 JANUARY 1649

Charles I (of England, Scotland and Ireland) is chiefly remembered for the English Civil War, in which he fought the forces of the English and Scottish Parliaments that had challenged his attempts to overrule parliamentary authority. Having been defeated, Charles was accused of treason by the republican victors and sentenced to death. His execution was set for early on the morning of 30 January 1649, although it had to be delayed while Parliament ensured it would be treason for anyone to proclaim a successor.

Charles I (1600–1649), King of England, Scotland, and Ireland, was born in Dunfermline Castle on 19 November 1600 and baptised at the Palace of Holyroodhouse, Edinburgh, the following month.

He succeeded his father, James VI and I, as King in 1625.

Charles prayed in the morning and dressed in two shirts so he would not shiver in the cold and appear frightened of his fate. The execution took place on a platform set against the wall of the Banqueting House on Whitehall (still standing), to which chains and manacles had been attached in case the King resisted execution. But showing considerable self-control, Charles not only remained calm but also delivered the following speech, in which he declared himself a 'martyr of the people'. He then forgave his executioner, said some more prayers and gave the signal that was to sever his head from his body.

I SHALL BE VERY LITTLE heard of anybody here… Indeed I could hold my peace very well, if I did not think that holding my peace would make some men think that I did submit to the guilt, as well as to the punishment; but I think it is my duty to God first, and to my country, for to clear myself both as an honest man, and a good King and a good Christian.

I shall begin first with my innocence. In troth I think it not very needful for me to insist upon this, for all the world knows that I never did begin a war with the two Houses of Parliament, and I call God to witness, to whom I must shortly make an account, that I never did intend for to encroach upon their privileges, they began upon me, it is the militia they began upon, they confess that the militia was mine, but they thought it fit for to have it from me.

I could hold my peace very well,
if I did not think that holding my peace would make
some think that I did submit to the guilt.

God forbid that I should be so ill a Christian, as not to say that God's judgments are just upon me: many times he does pay justice by an unjust sentence, that is ordinary: I will only say this, that an unjust sentence that I suffered to take effect, is punished now by an unjust sentence upon me, that is, so far I have said, to show you that I am an innocent man.

Now for to show you that I am a good Christian: I hope there is a good man that will bear me witness, that I have forgiven all the world, and even those in particular that have been the chief causers of my death: who they are, God knows, I do not desire to know, I pray God forgive them.

But this is not all, my charity must go farther, I wish that they may repent, for indeed they have committed a great sin in that particular: I pray God with St Stephen, that this be not laid to their charge, nay, not only so, but that they may take the right way to the peace of the kingdom, for my charity commands me not only to forgive particular men, but my charity commands me to endeavor to the last gasp the peace of the kingdom...

... for the people and truly I desire their liberty and freedom as much as any body whomsoever, but I must tell you, that their liberty and their freedom consists in having of Government; those laws, by which their life and their goods may be most of their own.

I have forgiven all the world, and even those in particular
that have been the chief causers of my death.

It is not for having share in government (Sir) that is nothing pertaining to them; a subject and a sovereign are clean different things, and therefore until they do that, I mean, that you do put the people in that liberty as I say, certainly they will never enjoy themselves. Sirs, it was for this that now I am come here: if I would have given way to an arbitrary way, for to have all laws changed according to the power of the sword, I needed not to have come here, and therefore I tell you (and I pray God it be not laid to your charge) that I am a martyr of the people.

In troth, Sirs, I shall not hold you much longer, for I will only say thus to you, that in truth I could have desired some little time longer, because I would have put then that I have said in a little more order, and a little better digested than I have done, and therefore I hope you will excuse me.

I have delivered my conscience, I pray God that you do take those courses that are best for the good of the kingdom, and your own salvation.

… In troth Sirs, my conscience in religion I think is very well known to all the

> My charity commands me to endeavor to the
> last gasp the peace of the kingdom.

world, and therefore I declare before you all, that I die a Christian, according to the profession of the Church of England, as I found it left me by my father, and this honest man I think will witness it.

… I have a good cause, and a gracious God on my side… I go from a corruptible to an incorruptible crown; where no disturbance can be, no disturbance in the world.

For none comes into the world with a saddle upon his back, neither any booted and spurred to ride him.

Richard Rumbold
c.1622–1685

SPEECH FROM THE SCAFFOLD · EDINBURGH

26 JUNE 1685

In early 1685 Richard Rumbold, who had been one of the guards surrounding the scaffold when Charles I was executed in January 1649, joined the Duke of Monmouth when the latter began preparing to depose the newly crowned James II. Argyll made him a colonel, and Rumbold successfully held off loyalist militia when Argyll, with the main force, tried to attack Inveraray.

Richard Rumbold was born around 1622 and served under Cromwell at Dunbar and Worcester. Despite losing an eye, he remained in the army throughout the 1650s, although by the 1670s Rumbold was rumoured to be involved in republican plots against the monarchy. He was indicted for treason following the Rye House Conspiracy in 1682, but escaped. He was hanged, drawn and quartered following the 1685 rebellion.

Luck, however, was not with the rebel forces. When they panicked as they crossed the River Clyde into Renfrewshire, Rumbold was dispatched to try and restore order. But discipline was poor, the force was fragmented and when the loyalist militia attacked the rebels they were completely routed.

Rumbold, who was badly wounded, was paraded through Edinburgh and, because of his injuries, was tried on 26 June 1685 and executed the same day. In this speech from the scaffold, he admitted his complicity in the rebellion but denied being a republican. Most memorable was his closing assertion of political equality:

'I am sure there was no man born marked of God above another, for none comes into the world with a saddle upon his back, neither any booted and spurred to ride him.'

IT IS FOR ALL men that come into the world once to die; and after death the judgment! And since death is a debt that all of us must pay, it is but a matter of small moment what way it be done. Seeing the Lord is pleased in this manner to take me to Himself, I confess, something hard to flesh and blood, yet blessed be His name, who hath made me not only willing, but thankful for His honouring me to lay down the life He gave, for His name; in which, were every hair in this head and beard of mine a life, I should joyfully sacrifice them for it, as I do this. Providence having brought me hither, I think it most necessary to clear myself of some aspersions laid upon my name; and, first, that I should have had so horrid an intention of destroying the king and his brother.

It was also laid to my charge that I was antimonarchical. It was ever my thoughts that kingly government was the best of all where justly executed; I mean, such as it was by our ancient laws – that is, a king, and a legal, free-chosen Parliament – the king having, as I conceive, power enough to make him great; the people also as much property as to make them happy; they being, as it were, contracted to one another! And who will deny me that this was not the

> ## Death is a debt that all of us must pay, it is but a matter of small moment what way it be done.

justly constituted government of our nation? How absurd is it, then, for men of sense to maintain that tho the one party of his contract break all conditions, the other should be obliged to perform their part? No; this error is contrary to the law of God, the law of nations, and the law of reason.

But as pride hath been the bait the devil hath caught most by ever since the creation, so it continues to this day with us. Pride caused our first parents to fall from the blessed state wherein they were created – they aiming to be higher and wiser than God allowed, which brought an everlasting curse on them and their posterity. It was pride caused God to drown the old world. And it was Nimrod's pride in building Babel that caused that heavy curse of division of tongues to be spread among us, as it is at this day, one of the greatest afflictions the Church of God groaneth under, that there should be so many divisions during their pilgrimage here; but this is their comfort that the day draweth near where, as there is but one shepherd, there shall be but one sheepfold. It was, therefore, in the defence of this party, in their just rights and liberties, against popery and slavery! I die this day in defence of the ancient laws and liberties of these nations; and tho God, for reasons best known to Himself, hath not seen it fit to honour us, as to make us the instruments for the deliverance of His people, yet as I have lived, so I die in the faith that He will speedily arise for the deliverance of His

> ## I think it most important to clear myself of some aspersions laid upon my name; and, first, that I should have had so horrid an intention of destroying the king and his brother.

Church and people. And I desire of all you to prepare for this with speed. I may say this is a deluded generation, veiled with ignorance, that tho popery and slavery be riding in upon them, do not perceive it; tho I am sure there was no man born marked of God above another, for none comes into the world with a saddle on his back, neither any booted and spurred to ride him. Not but that I am well satisfied that God hath wisely ordered different stations for men in the world, as I have already said; kings having as much power as to make them great and the people as much property as to make them happy. And to conclude, I shall only add my wishes for the salvation of all men who were created for that end.

None can destroy Scotland, save Scotland itself; hold your Hands from the Pen, you are secure.

Lord Belhaven
1656–1708

SPEECH TO THE OLD SCOTTISH PARLIAMENT · EDINBURGH

2 NOVEMBER 1706

Lord Belhaven was perhaps one of the most vocal opponents of the Treaty of Union between Scotland and England as it passed through the old Scottish parliament. On 2 November 1706 he delivered his famous 'Mother Caledonia' speech opposing the Union, an emotional survey of Scottish history, constantly beginning sentences with the phrase 'I think I see' in order to spell out what he believed Scotland would lose by giving up its sovereignty.

Some lines jar today, such as the Kirk 'voluntarily descending into a Plain, upon an equal Level with Jews [and] Papists', and indeed the speech was ridiculed by political contemporaries. Patrick Hume, the 1st Earl of Marchmont, scathingly commented, 'Behold, he dreamed, but lo! when he awoke, he found it a dream', while Lord Seafield told a correspondent that 'My Lord Belhaven had a speech contrived to incense the common people; it had no great influence in the House'.

From 4 November 1706, Belhaven voted consistently against the articles of the Treaty of Union and, on 16 January 1707, voted against ratifying the Treaty itself.

John Hamilton, 2nd Lord Belhaven and Stenton was born in Edinburgh in 1656, the eldest son of Lord Presmennan, a Court of Session judge. He attended the 1685 and 1686 Scottish parliaments, and Balhaven was one of the Scottish nobles who, in January 1689, invited William of Orange to assume the government of Scotland. He fought 'bravely' in the Battle of Killiecrankie and later became a privy councillor.

MY LORD CHANCELLOR, when I consider the Affair of an Union betwixt the two Nations, as it is expressed in the several Articles thereof, and now the Subject of our Deliberation at this Time; I find my Mind crouded with Variety of melancholy thoughts, and I think it my Duty to disburden myself of some of them, by laying them before, and exposing them to the serious Consideration of this honourable House.

I think I see a free and independent Kingdom delivering up that, which all the

World hath been fighting for since the Days of Nimrod; yea, that for which most of all the Empires, Kingdoms, States, Principalities, and Dukedoms of Europe, are at this time engaged in the most bloody and cruel Wars that ever were, to wit, a Power to manage their own Affairs by themselves, without the Assistance and Counsel of any other.

I think I see a national Church, founded upon a Rock, secured by a Claim of Right, hedged and fenced about, by the strictest and most pointed, legal Sanction that Sovereignty could contrive, voluntarily descending into a Plain, upon an equal Level with Jews, Papists, Socinians, Arminians, Anabaptists, and other Sectaries, &c.

I think I see the noble and honourable Peerage of Scotland, whose valiant Predecessors led Armies against their Enemies, upon their own proper Charges and Expences, now divested of their Followers and Vassalages, and put upon such an equal Foot with their Vassals, that I think I see a petty English Exciseman receive more Homage and Respect than what was paid formerly to their quondam Mackallamores.

> I think I see a free and independent kingdom delivering up that, which all the world hath been fighting for since the Days of Nimrod.

I think I see the present Peers of Scotland, whose noble Ancestors conquered Provinces, over-run Countries, reduced and subjected Towns and fortified Places, exacted Tribute through the greatest Part of England, now walking in the Court of Requests like so many English Attorneys, laying aside their Walking Swords when in Company with the English Peers, lest their Self-defence should be found Murder.

I think I see the honourable Estate of Barons, the bold Assertors of the Nation's Rights and Liberties in the worst of Times, now setting a Watch upon their Lips, and a Guard upon their Tongues, lest they be found guilty of Scandalum Magnatum.

I think I see the Royal State of Boroughs walking their desolate Streets, hanging down their Heads under Disappointment, wormed out of all the Branches of their old Trade, uncertain what Hand to turn to, necessitate to become 'Prentices to their unkind Neighbours; and yet after all, finding their Trade so fortified by Companies, and secured by Prescriptions, that they despair of any Success therein.

I think I see our learned Judges laying aside their Practiques and Decisions, studying the Common Law of England, gravelled with Certioraries, Nisi Prius's, Writs of Error, Verdicts Indovar, Ejectione Firmae, Injunctions, Demurs, &c. and frighted with Appeals and Avocations, because of the new Regulations and Rectifications they may meet with.

I think I see the valiant and gallant Soldiery either sent to learn the Plantation-Trade abroad; or at home petitioning for a small Subsistance, as a Reward of their honourable Exploits; while their old Corps are broken, the common Soldiers left to beg, and the youngest English Corps kept standing.

I think I see the honest industrious Tradesman loaded with new Taxes and Impositions, disappointed of the Equivalents, drinking Water in place of Ale, eating his saltless Pottage, petitioning for Encouragement to his Manufactures, and answered by Counter-Petitions.

> *I see our ancient Mother Caledonia,*
> *like Caesar, sitting in the midst of our senate,*
> *ruefully looking around her, covering herself*
> *with her royal Garment, attending the final Blow.*

In short, I think I see the laborious Ploughman, with his Corn spoiling upon his Hands, for want of Sale, cursing the Day of his Birth, dreading the Expence of his Burial, and uncertain whether to marry or do worse.

I think I see the incurable Difficulties of the Landed Men, fettered under the golden Chain of Equivalents, their pretty Daughters petitioning for want of Husbands, and their Sons for want of Employment.

I think I see our Mariners delivering up their Ships to their Dutch Partners; and what through Presses and Necessity, earning their Bread as Underlings in the royal English Navy.

But above all, my Lord, I think I see our ancient Mother Caledonia, like Caesar, sitting in the midst of our Senate, ruefully looking round about her, covering herself with her royal Garment, attending the fatal Blow, and breathing out her last with an Et tu quoque mi fili.

> *Should not the Consideration of these Things*
> *vivify these dry Bones of ours? Should not the memory*
> *of our noble predecessors Valour and Constancy*
> *rouze up our drooping spirirts?*

Are not these, my Lord, very afflicting Thoughts? And yet they are but the least Part suggested to me by these dishonourable Articles. Should not the Consideration of these Things vivify these dry Bones of ours? Should not the Memory of our noble Predecessors Valour and Constancy rouze up our drooping Spirits? Are our noble Predecessors Souls got so far into the English Cabbage-stock and Colliflowers, that we should shew the least Inclination that way?

Are our Eyes so blinded? Are our Ears so deafned? Are our Hearts so hardened?
Are our Tongues so faltered? Are our Hands so settered, that in this our Day,
I say, my Lord, that in this our Day, we should not mind the Things that concern
the very Being and Well-being of our ancient Kingdom, before the Day be hid
from our Eyes?

No, my Lord, God forbid! Man's Extremity is God's Opportunity: He is a
present Help in time of need, and a Deliverer, and that right early. Some
unforeseen Providence will fall out, that may cast the Balance; some Joseph or
other will say, Why do ye strive together, since you are Brethren?

None can destroy Scotland, save Scotland itself; hold your Hands from the
Pen, you are secure. Some Judah or other will say, Let not our Hands be upon the
Lad, he is our Brother. There will be a Jehovah Jireh, and some Ram will be
caught in the Thicket, when the bloody Knife is at our Mother's Throat. Let us up
then, my Lord, and let our noble Patriots behave themselves like Men, and we
know not how soon a Blessing may come.

I was brought up in true, loyal, and anti-revolution principles.

Lord Balmerino
1688–1746

SPEECH FROM THE SCAFFOLD • LONDON

18 AUGUST 1746

Lord Balmerino was a Jacobite army officer, the first to take his troops into Derby during the 1745 uprising. The following year, when the Jacobites were defeated at Culloden, it was Balmerino who helped Bonnie Prince Charlie away from his post as cannonballs fell around the Stuart standard.

Following the defeat, Balmerino gave himself up the next day and was brought to trial with the Earls of Kilmarnock and Cromarty at Westminster Hall on a charge of high treason. He pleaded not guilty, arguing that he was not present at Carlisle at the time specified in the indictment. Sent to the Tower of London, Balmerino was brought up for trial the next day and conducted his own, rather futile, defence. Unlike the two earls, he declined to sue for mercy.

Arthur Elphinstone was born in 1688, son of John Elphinstone, the 4th Lord Balmerino. Despite his Episcopalian background, Elphinstone accepted a commission under Queen Anne but subsequently deserted to the Jacobites. He had to flee the country after the 1715 rising, remaining in France until 1734, when he was pardoned. He was executed in 1746, following the second Jacobite uprising.

On the day of his execution, Balmerino gave his executioner, John Thrift, a fee of three guineas, although it still required three blows to sever his head. This is his defiant speech from the scaffold. His final words were apparently 'God preserve my *Friends*, forgive my *Enemies*, restore the *KING*, and have Mercy upon my *Soul!*'

I WAS BROUGHT UP IN TRUE, loyal, and anti-revolution principles, and I hope the world is convinced that they stick to me.

I must acknowledge I did a very inconsiderate thing, for which I am heartily sorry, in accepting of a company of foot [soldiers] from the Princess Anne, who I knew had no more right to the crown than her predecessor the Prince of Orange, whom I always look upon as a vile, unnatural usurper.

To make amends for what I had done I joined the King when he was in Scotland, and when all was over I made my escape and lived abroad till the year 1734.

In the beginning of that year I got a letter from my father which very much surprised me. It was to let me know that he had got the promise of a remission for me. I did not know what to do. I was then, I think, in the Canton of Bern and had nobody to advise with. But next morning I wrote a letter to the King, who was then at Rome, to acquaint His Majesty that this was done without my asking or knowledge, and that I would not accept of without His Majesty's consent. I had in answer to mine a letter written with the King's own hand allowing me to go home, and he told me his banker would give me money for my travelling charges when I came to Paris, which accordingly I got.

When His Royal Highness came to Edinburgh, as it was my bounden and indispensible duty, I joined him, though I might easily have excused myself from taking arms on account of my age. But I never could have had peace of conscience if I had stayed at home when that brave Prince was exposing himself to all manner of dangers and fatigue both night and day.

> *I am convinced that it is a malicious report industriously spread to excuse themselves of the murders they were guilty of in calm blood after the battle.*

I am at a loss when I come to speak of the Prince; I am not a fit hand to draw his character. I shall leave that to others. But I must beg leave to tell you the incomparable sweetness of his nature, his affability, his compassion, his justice, his temperance, his patience, and his courage are virtues seldom all to be found in one person. In short, he wants no qualifications requisite to make a great man.

Pardon me, if I say, wherever I had the command I never suffered any disorders to be committed, as will appear by the Duke of Buccleuch's servants at East Park, by the Earl of Findlater's minister, Mr Lato, and my Lord's servants at Cullen, by Mr Rose, minister at Nairn, who was pleased to favour me with a visit when I was a prisoner in Inverness, by Mr Stewart, principal servant to the Lord President at the house of Culloden, and by several other people. All this gives me great pleasure now that I am looking on the block on which I am ready to lay down my head. And though it had not been my own natural inclination to protect every body as far as lay in my power it would have been my interest so to do. For His Royal Highness abhorred all those who were capable of doing injustice to any of the King, his father's subjects, whatever opinion they were of.

I have heard since I came to this place that there has been a most wicked report spread and mentioned in several of the newspapers, that His Royal Highness, the Prince, before the Battle of Culloden, had given out in orders that no quarters should be given to the enemy. This is such an unchristian thing and so unlike that gallant Prince that nobody that knows him will believe it. It is very strange if there had been any such orders that neither the Earl of Kilmarnock, who was Colonel of the Regiment of Foot-guards, nor I, who was Colonel of the 2nd Troop of Life-guards, should never have heard anything of it, especially since we were both at the head-quarters the morning before the battle. I am convinced that it is a malicious report industriously spread to excuse themselves for the murders they were guilty of in calm blood after the battle.

> I was brought up in true,
> loyal and anti-revolution principles,
> and I hope the world is convinced that they stick to me.

Ever since my confinement in the Tower, when Major White and Mr Fowler did me the honour of a vist, their behaviour was always so kind and obliging to me that I cannot find words to express it. But I am sorry I cannot say the same thing of General Williamson. He has treated me barbarously, but not quite so ill as he did the Bishop of Rochester. I forgive him and all my enemies. Had it not been for Mr Gordon's advice I should have prayed for him as David does, Psalm 109.

I hope you will have the charity to believe I die in peace with all men, for yesterday I received the Holy Eucharist from the hands of a clergyman of the Church of England, in whose Communion I die as in union with the Episcopal Church of Scotland.

I shall conclude with a short prayer.

O Almighty God! I humbly beseech Thee to bless the King, the Prince, and Duke of York, and all the dutiful branches of the Royal Family! Endue them with thy Holy Spirit, enrich them with thy heavenly grace, prosper them with all happiness and bring them to thine everlasting kingdom! Finally I recommend to thy fatherly goodness all my benefactors and all the faithful adherents to the cause for which I am now about to suffer. God reward them! Make them happy here and in the world to come! This I beg for Christ's sake, in whose words, etc. Our Father, etc.

The History of the World...
is the Biography of Great Men.

Thomas Carlyle
1795–1881

LECTURE ON 'THE HERO AS DIVINITY' • LONDON

5 MAY 1840

The great Victorian writer, historian and biographer Thomas Carlyle spent the winter and spring of 1840 working on what he vowed would be his last series of lectures. With a biography of Oliver Cromwell in mind, Carlyle used these speeches to articulate the central theses of a new book, *On Heroes, Hero-Worship, and the Heroic in History*, which was published the following year.

Thomas Carlyle was born in 1795 in Ecclefechan, Dumfriesshire, the eldest son of a stonemason. Educated at Annan Academy and Edinburgh University, he later became a teacher, married and, in the mid-1820s, turned increasingly to writing. Carlyle moved to London in 1834, beginning work on a history of the French Revolution, the first of numerous volumes of history, biography and commentary. He died in 1881.

This first lecture, on 'The Hero as Divinity', demonstrates the scope of Carlyle's powerful rhetoric, in which he posited that history depended on the role of the strong man. Always fascinated by the relationship between spiritual and secular power, Carlyle believed that men such as Napoleon and Cromwell had succeeded as leaders by incorporating in their conscious and unconscious acts central spiritual truths.

Carlyle had started lecturing in 1837, chiefly to win influence and earn a living. His style was nervous, eccentric, even extravagant, but audiences flocked to hear him speak. At the end of April 1838 he gave the first of 12 lectures on European literature, and lectured again in the spring of 1839, and the spring of 1840.

WE HAVE UNDERTAKEN TO discourse here for a little on Great Men, their manner of appearance in our world's business, how they have shaped themselves in the world's history, what ideas men formed of them, what work they did; – on Heroes, namely, and on their reception and performance; what I call Hero-worship and the Heroic in human affairs...

We cannot look, however imperfectly, upon a great man, without gaining something by him. He is the living light-fountain, which it is good and pleasant to be near. The light which enlightens, which has enlightened the darkness of the world; and this not as a kindled lamp only, but rather as a natural luminary shining by the gift of Heaven; a flowing light-fountain, as I say, of native original insight, of manhood and heroic nobleness; – in whose radiance all souls feel that it is well with them. On any terms whatsoever, you will not grudge to wander in such neighbourhood for a while...

The young generations of the world, who had in them the freshness of young children, and yet the depth of earnest men, who did not think that they had finished off all things in Heaven and Earth by merely giving them scientific names, but had to gaze direct at them there, with awe and wonder: they felt better what of divinity is in man and Nature; they, without being mad, could worship Nature, and man more than anything else in Nature. Worship, that is, as I said above, admire without limit: this, in the full use of their faculties, with all sincerity of heart, they could do. I consider Hero-worship to be the grand modifying element in that ancient system of thought. What I called the perplexed jungle of Paganism sprang, we may say, out of many roots: every admiration, adoration of a star or natural object, was a root or fibre of a root; but Hero-worship is the deepest root of all; the tap-root, from which in a great degree all the rest were nourished and grown.

No nobler feeling than this of admiration, submission, burning, boundless, for a noblest godlike form of Man, is not that the gem of Christianity itself?

And now if worship even of a star had some meaning in it, how much more might that of a Hero! Worship of a Hero is transcendent admiration of a Great Man. I say great men are still admirable; I say there is, at bottom, nothing else admirable! No nobler feeling than this of admiration for one higher than himself dwells in the breast of man. It is to this hour, and at all hours, the vivifying influence in man's life. Religion I find stand upon it; not Paganism only, but far higher and truer religions, – all religion hitherto known. Hero-worship, heartfelt prostrate admiration, submission, burning, boundless, for a noblest godlike Form of Man, – is not that the germ of Christianity itself? The greatest of all Heroes is One – whom we do not name here! Let sacred silence meditate that sacred matter; you will find it the ultimate perfection of a principle extant throughout man's whole history on earth...

I am well aware that in these days Hero-worship, the thing I call Hero-worship, professes to have gone out, and finally ceased. This, for reasons which it will be worth while some time to inquire into, is an age that as it were denies the existence of great men; denies the desirableness of great men. Show our critics a great man, a Luther for example, they begin to what they call 'account' for him; not to worship him, but take the dimensions of him, – and bring him out to be a little kind of man! He was the 'creature of the Time', they say; the Time called him forth, the Time did everything, he nothing – but what we the little critic could have done too! This seems to me but melancholy work.

The Time call forth? Alas, we have known Times call loudly enough for their great man; but not find him when they called! He was not there; Providence had not sent him; the Time, calling its loudest, had to go down to confusion and wreck because he would not come when called.

And now if worship even of a star had some meaning in it, how much more might that of a Hero!

For if we will think of it, no Time need have gone to ruin, could it have found a man great enough, a man wise and good enough: wisdom to discern truly what the Time wanted, valor to lead it on the right road thither; these are the salvation of any Time. But I liken common languid Times, with their unbelief, distress, perplexity, with their languid doubting characters and embarrassed circumstances, impotently crumbling down into ever worse distress towards final ruin; – all this I liken to dry dead fuel, waiting for the lightning out of Heaven that shall kindle it. The great man, with his free force direct out of God's own hand, is the lightning. His word is the wise healing word which all can believe in. All blazes round him now, when he has once struck on it, into fire like his own. The dry mouldering sticks are thought to have called him forth. They did want him greatly; but as to calling him forth – ! Those are critics of small vision, I think, who cry: 'See, is it not the sticks that made the fire?' No sadder proof can be given by a man of his own littleness than disbelief in great men. There is no sadder symptom of a generation than such general blindness to the spiritual lightning, with faith only in the heap of barren dead fuel. It is the last consummation of unbelief. In all epochs of the world's history, we shall find the Great Man to have been the indispensable savior of his epoch; – the lightning, without which the fuel never would have burnt. The History of the World, I said already, was the Biography of Great Men.

We quit a vitiated Establishment – but we shall rejoice to return to a poorer one.

Thomas Chalmers
1780–1847

SPEECH TO INAUGURAL GENERAL ASSEMBLY OF THE
FREE CHURCH OF SCOTLAND • TANFIELD HALL • EDINBURGH

18 MAY 1843

The Disruption of 1843 was both a tragedy and a triumph, the former because it brought to an end the unity of the national Church of Scotland as enshrined in the Treaty of Union with England, and the latter because it was a dramatic assertion of the Kirk's independence. At a basic level – and the events surrounding the Disruption were anything but simple – it hinged upon the rights of congregations to have a say in the selection of their ministers.

After years of lobbying Westminster, the General Assembly sent Parliament a final appeal for the recognition of its spiritual independence in May 1842. Seven months later the Tory government of Sir Robert Peel rejected the Kirk's appeal while the Court of Session imposed a large fine on the presbytery of Auchterarder for its continued refusal to ordain a vetoed minister.

During the General Assembly of May 1843, therefore, Thomas Chalmers led around 470 ministers, more than a third of the Kirk's total, and around half the lay membership, out of St Andrew's Church on Edinburgh's George Street to the Tanfield Hall in order to constitute the Free Church of Scotland. He became its first moderator and this is from his first speech to that historic Assembly.

Thomas Chalmers was born in 1780 in Anstruther, Fife, the son of a local merchant and provost. He was educated locally and at the University of St Andrews, becoming a minister soon after graduating. Chalmers studied philosophy, wrote about politics and ministered (not very well) in Kilmany. In 1811 he became an evangelical, eventually leading that grouping in the General Assembly of the Church of Scotland. He died in 1847.

AND NOW, REVEREND FATHERS and brethren, it is well that you should have been strengthened by your Master in Heaven to make the surrender you have done of everything that is dear to nature; – casting aside all your earthly dependence rather than offend conscience, incur the guilt of sinful compliance by thwarting your own sense of duty, and running counter to the Bible, our Great

Church Directory and Statute Book. It is well that you have made for the present a clean escape from this condemnation – and that in the issue of the contest between a sacrifice of principle and a sacrifice of your worldly possessions, you have resolved upon the latter; and while to the eye of sense you are without a provision and a home, embarked upon a wide ocean of uncertainty, have that great and generous certainty which is apprehended by the eye of faith, that God reigneth, and that he will not forsake the families of the faithful...

> But let us preserve in administering
> the affairs of the Church without fear and without
> flattery – not fearing men but God.

By giving up our connection with the State, and by separating ourselves from the worldly advantages connected therewith, we may be said to have withstood one temptation – but such is the deceitfulness of the human heart, that without paying great heed to the exhortations which the Apostles pressed upon their early converts, there is danger of our being carried in another form, and by another temptation, to the same sin. Rather than be seduced from our great principles, we give up all our earthly dependence; but let principle have her perfect work, and let us have a care lest we lie tempted to give up another principle by promoting and encouraging reliance on another dependence. Rather than compromise the authority of Christ's Church, you have forfeited the countenance of men in power – that is, of the men who are now in possession of the high places of the State...

In a word, we hold that every post and function of the Commonwealth should be leavened with Christianity, and that every functionary, from the highest to the lowest, should in their respective spheres, do all that in them lies to countenance and to uphold it. That is to say, though we quit the Establishment, it is right that it should be understood that we go out holding the Establishment principle. We quit a vitiated Establishment – but we shall rejoice to return to a poorer one. (Great applause.) Or to express it otherwise, we advocate the national recognition and the national support of religion, and we are not Voluntaries...

> In the issue of the contest between a sacrifice of principle
> and a sacrifice of your worldly possessions,
> you have resolved upon the latter.

Let us turn now to those that are within – to our people and to those who adhere to the principles for which we contend in the Free Presbyterian Church which we this day institute in these lands. We know the taunts of those who speak reproachfully, that though the word 'free' is emblazoned on the title of our

Church, we shall find it an empty name – that instead of being subject to the restraints of a lawful authority, we shall have the more galling and more intolerable tyranny of a multitude – as if there was no possible way of holding steadfast truth and principle in opposition to both – as if there was no possibility of being guided by Scripture and common sense to refuse all sinful, and, let me add, senseless compliances with either. None will deny that the first teachers of

> *There is a danger of our being carried in another form, and by another temptation, to the same sin.*

Christianity cleared their way independently on all hands. They had, indeed, the voice of inspiration; and why may not we do the same, who walk by no light and submit to no authority in spiritual things, but the light and the authority of that enduring book the Bible – the common statute for both ministers and people...

Let us arm ourselves with the same mind; and, fresh from the sacrifice we have already made, rather than surrender the powers of our office, let us be prepared to make like sacrifice in other quarters – the loss of popularity and good will. But let us persevere in administering the affairs of the Church without fear and without flattery – not fearing men but God. (Cheers.)

If there was to be found a house open for him, he would yet raise the cry 'send back the blood-stained dollars'

Frederick Douglass
1818–1895

'THE FREE CHURCH OF SCOTLAND
AND AMERICAN SLAVERY' ADDRESS • DUNDEE
30 JANUARY 1846

The American social reformer and anti-slavery campaigner arrived in Liverpool on 28 August 1845 and spent the next 18 months travelling extensively in Britain and Ireland, giving well-attended lectures in dozens of cities and towns. He spent most of the first half of 1846 in Scotland, and liked it so much he returned three times later that same year. Home to some of the more radical anti-slavery sentiment, Scotland gave Douglass a warm response, responding well to his powerful and charismatic oratory which, back in the US, many found hard to believe came from a former slave.

Frederick Douglass (born Frederick Augustus Washington Bailey) was born in 1818. After escaping from slavery he became a leader of the abolitionist movement, achieving fame for his sparkling oratory and incisive writing style. He published several autobiographies and died in 1895.

His speeches condemned American slavery and suggested how Scots could aid the movement calling for its abolition. But he was also keen to identify those who seemed to undermine this strategy, and the main target on his Scottish tour was the Free Church of Scotland. Deprived of money following its split from the Kirk in 1843, this breakaway church had sought to raise funds among friendly Presbyterians in the United States, including some from churches in the slaveholding South.

Interpreting this as an uncritical endorsement of the churches there, who refused to condemn slavery or expel slaveholding members, a campaign calling for the Free Church to return this money was well under way by the time Douglass set foot in Scotland. But his oratory electrified the campaign, with the slogan 'Send Back the Money' even being carved out of the turf on Arthur's Seat in Edinburgh, as well as inspiring several songs.

DOES THE FREE CHURCH represent your views on the question of slavery? (Cries of no! no!) I am glad to hear it. They claim to be the model, the impersonation, the life, the soul of Christianity in this country. Well, with all these influences, and with their exceedingly tender consciences, (laughter) and with professions of love to God and man, they leave their homes and go to the United States, and strike hands in good Christian fellowship with men whose hands are full of blood – the coats, the boots, the watches, the houses, and all they possess, are the result of the unpaid toil of the poor fettered, stricken, and branded slave. Where did these parties go when they went to the United States? I want to ask Mr Lewis where he went? (Great cheering and a few hisses.)

> ## If slaveholding is a sin,
> ## as they admit it is, it is a sin in any circumstances.

I am glad to hear these hisses. It was said by a very learned man that when the cool voice of truth falls into the burning vortex of falsehood there would always be hissing. Innocence fears nothing. Perfect love casts off all fear. Innocence rusheth into the sunlight, and asks to be tried. It does not slink away and hide. It does not apologise and say I cannot talk with this or that man, because I do not know if he sustains an excellent reputation. It has no fears of this kind, it seeks to be searched and tried; and if there is a man here who feels for a moment that I should not unmask the Free Church of Scotland, he has more love for his sect than for truth, more love for his religious denomination than for God. I ought to have asked the brother who hissed, did not brother Lewis go to the United States? Did he not take the slaveholders' money, and put it into his pocket? Let him come here and defend himself...

The question with the Free Church is very easily settled if divested of all their sophistries. Their first justification is that the slaveholders are so situated that they cannot help holding their slaves; they are compelled by the laws of the land to hold them. I am here to pronounce this utterly false. There is not a slaveholder in the United States but can set his slaves free. In all the states except three, they can be set free on the soil. In three, I admit they cannot be set free on the soil unless the slaveholder becomes responsible for their good behaviour, but he can

> ## If there is a man here who feels for a moment
> ## that I should not unmask the Free Church of Scotland,
> ## he has more love for his sect than for the truth.

convey them to the protection of the British lion which prowls on three sides of them. But even if this were the case, it would not justify them. If slaveholding is a sin, as they admit it is, it is a sin in any circumstances...

He would read from the New Orleans Picayune of 7 July 1845, a paper
notorious for its slaveholding, slave-trading, slave-selling, and slave-buying
tendencies, a eulogy on the Rev Dr Chalmers for his course on the slavery
question, and on another page of the same paper was an advertisement for two
run-away negroes. The paragraph was as follows:

'Dr Chalmers, the eloquent Scotch divine, having been appealed to by the
members of the Free Church of Scotland, on the subject of receiving contributions
from churches in the slave states of America, to say whether religious fellowship
could consistently be extended to slaveholding churches, the Doctor repudiates
the spirit that would narrow the sphere of Christian union, and says, that the
refusal of such fellowship would be "most unjustifiable".'

Innocence rusheth into the sunlight, and asks to be tried.

Fellowship with slaveholders! – refuse fellowship with man-stealers,
woman-whippers, cradle-robbers, and plunderers! – to refuse Christian
fellowship with such would be 'most unjustifiable.' (Applause.) Did they think
Dr Chalmers would ever have said this, if, like him, he had had four sisters and
one brother in bondage? (Cheers, and cries of 'No.') Would this paper have
eulogised George Thompson or William Lloyd Garrison, or any other eminent
abolitionist? (No, no!)...

He concluded by making an earnest and eloquent appeal to the people of
Scotland to lend their assistance in freeing three million of their fellow creatures
from bondage. Let the people of Scotland arise, and show the Free Church that
they did not represent them. Let the voice of public opinion compel that church
to send back the money. He would again visit Dundee, where, if there was to be
found a house open for him, he would yet raise the cry 'send back the blood-
stained dollars'. (Great cheering.)

You are invited and encouraged by the prosecutor to snap the thread of that young life.

John Inglis
1810–1891

SPEECH AT TRIAL OF MADELEINE SMITH • EDINBURGH

8 JULY 1857

John Inglis (later Lord Glencorse) was already a star of the Faculty of Advocates by the time his public reputation was sealed with this defence of Madeleine Smith at a celebrated trial in 1857. Charged with poisoning an intimate acquaintance, Smith was defended by Inglis against a formidable prosecution team.

Although circumstantial evidence pointed towards Smith's guilt, Inglis closed his case with a long and impressive speech that succeeded in breaking through the web of circumstantial evidence woven by the prosecution. Inglis' 'spontaneous movements seem to sympathise with the current and the emphasis of his argument'.[3]

The speech, although it became widely known and very popular, did not, according to a biographer, 'give the same assurance of gigantic intellect as did many of his extempore speeches in the Inner House'.[4] Nevertheless, the jury delivered a 'not proven' verdict, and Smith left Scotland a free woman.

John Inglis, Lord Glencorse, was born in Edinburgh in 1810, a son of the manse. Educated at Edinburgh High School and the Universities of Glasgow and Oxford, he joined the Faculty of Advocates in 1835. A Conservative, he served as solicitor general and Lord Advocate and entered Parliament in 1858. That year he also became Lord Justice-Clerk and took the title Lord Glencorse. He died in 1891.

GENTLEMEN OF THE JURY, the charge against the prisoner is murder, and the punishment of murder is death: and that simple statement is sufficient to suggest to us the awful solemnity of the occasion which brings you and me face to face. But, gentlemen, there are peculiarities in the present case of so singular a kind – there is such an air of romance and mystery investing it from beginning to end – there is something so touching and exciting in the age, and the sex, and the social position of the accused – aye, and I must add, the public attention is so directed to the trial that they watch our proceedings and hang on our very accents with such an anxiety and eagerness of expectation, that I feel almost bowed down and overwhelmed by the magnitude of the task that is

imposed on me. You are invited and encouraged by the prosecutor to snap the
thread of that young life, and to consign to an ignominious death on the scaffold
one who, within a few short months, was known only as a gentle, confiding,
and affectionate girl, the ornament and pride of her happy home. Gentlemen,
the tone in which my learned friend the Lord Advocate addressed you yesterday
could not fail to strike you as most remarkable. It was characterised by great
moderation – by such moderation as I think must have convinced you that he
could hardly expect a verdict at your hands; and in the course of that address,
for which I gave him the highest credit, he could resist the expression of his own
deep feeling of commiseration for the position in which the prisoner is placed
– an involuntary homage paid by the official prosecutor to the kind and generous
nature of the man. But, gentlemen, I am going to ask you for something very
different from commiseration; I am going to ask you for that which I will not
condescend to be, but which I will loudly and importunately demand – that to
which every person is entitled, whether she be the lowest and vilest of her sex or
the maiden whose purity is as the unsunned snow. I ask you for justice; and if you
will kindly lend me your attention for the requisite period, and if Heaven grant
me patience and strength for the task, I shall tear to tatters that web of sophistry
in which the prosecutor has striven to involve this poor girl and her sad and
strange story...

> I shall tear to tatters that web of sophistry in which the
> prosecutor has striven to involve this poor girl.

... I have thus laid before you what I conceive to be all the important branches
of this inquiry separately, and as calmly and deliberately as I could; and I now
ask your judgement – I ask you to bring the whole powers with which God has
endowed you to the performance of this most solemn duty. I have heard it said
that juries have nothing to do with the consequences of their verdicts, and that
all questions of evidence must be weighed in the same scale, whether the crime
be a capital one or only penal in a lower degree. I cannot too indignantly
repudiate that doctrine. It may suit well enough the cramped mind of a legal
pedant, or the leaden rules of a heartless philosophy; but he maintains it is
entirely ignorant of the materials of which a jury ought to be and is composed.
Gentlemen, you are brought here for the performance of this great duty, not
because you have any particular skill in the sifting or weighing of evidence – not
because your intellects have been highly cultivated for that or similar purposes
– not because you are of a class or caste set apart for the work; but you are here
because, as the law expresses it, you are indifferent men – because you are like,
not because you are unlike, other men; not merely because you have clear heads,
but because you have also warm and tender hearts – because you have bosoms
filled with the same feelings and emotions, and because you entertain the same

sympathies and sentiments, as those whose lives, characters, and fortunes are placed in your hands...

The recollection of this day and this prisoner would haunt me as a dismal and blighting spectre to the end of life.

I say... ponder well before you permit anything short of the clearest evidence to seduce or mislead you into giving such an awful verdict as is demanded of you. Dare any man hearing me – dare any man here or elsewhere, say that he has formed a clear opinion against the prisoner – will any man venture for one moment to make that assertion? And yet, if on anything short of clear opinion you convict the prisoner, reflect – I beseech you reflect – what the consequences may be. Never did I feel so unwilling to part with a jury – never did I feel as if I had said so little, as I feel now after this long address. I cannot explain it to myself, except by a strong and overwhelming conviction of what your verdict ought to be. I am deeply conscious of a personal interest in your verdict, for if there should be any failure of justice, I could attribute it to no other cause than my own inability to conduct the defence; and I am persuaded that, if it were so, the recollection of this day and this prisoner would haunt me as a dismal and blighting spectre to the end of life. May the Spirit of all Truth guide you to an honest, a just, and a true verdict! But no verdict will be either honest, or just, or true, unless it at once satisfy the reasonable scruples of the severest judgement, and yet leave undisturbed and unvexed the tenderest conscience among you.

Go into the lofty hills of Afghanistan.

William Gladstone
1809–1898

SPEECH DURING MIDLOTHIAN CAMPAIGN • FORESTERS' HALL • DALKEITH
26 NOVEMBER 1879

Following his defeat at the general election 1874, Gladstone – the 'Grand Old Man' of British politics – resigned the Liberal leadership and, in his 60s, hoped to spend the rest of his life in retirement. The Balkan Massacres of 1876, however, drew him back to politics in protest at what he saw as an inadequate response from Benjamin Disraeli, his successor as Prime Minister, and also from his own party.

William Ewart Gladstone was born in 1809 to Scottish parents, although he was raised in Liverpool. Initially a Tory, he first entered Parliament in 1832 and in a career lasting more than six decades served as Chancellor four times, as well as Prime Minister in four different administrations. In 1886 Gladstone's policy of Irish Home Rule split the Liberal Party, and he resigned as premier in 1894. He died in 1898.

Having indicated his intention to retire from his Greenwich constituency in 1878, Gladstone chose the Conservative constituency of Midlothian, the county surrounding the city of Edinburgh, as a likely prospect. His anger at Conservative financial and foreign policies was to be the driving force of what became known as 'the Midlothian campaign', a series of speeches that denounced Disraeli and his record in government.

The following speech was delivered at the Foresters Hall in Dalkeith in 1879. The audiences for these speeches sometimes ran into the thousands, but for this oration it was a more modest 750. At its heart was an assault on colonial wars through which Gladstone's humanitarianism and tolerance for other races shone through. After a vote of thanks, the Grand Old Man left Dalkeith, passing rows of torchbearers who illuminated the streets in his honour. At the general election the following year, Gladstone was returned comfortably in the constituency.

GO FROM SOUTH AFRICA to the mountains of Central Asia. Go into the lofty hills of Afghanistan, as they were last winter, and what do we there see? I fear a yet sadder sight than was to be seen in the land of the Zulus. It is true that with respect to the operations of the war in Afghanistan you have seen none but official accounts, or hardly any but official accounts; and many of the facts belonging to that war have not been brought under the general notice of the British public. I think that a great misfortune...

What we know is this, that our gallant troops have been called upon to ascend to an elevation of many thousand feet, and to operate in the winter months I am going back to a period of nine or 12 months amidst the snows of winter. We know that that was done for the most part not strictly in the territory of Afghanistan proper, but in its border lands, inhabited by hill tribes who enjoy more or less of political independence, and do not owe a regular allegiance to the Afghan ruler. You have seen during last winter from time to time that from such and such a village attacks had been made upon the British forces, and that in consequence the village had been burned. Have you ever reflected on the meaning of these words? Do not suppose that I am pronouncing a censure, for I am not, either upon the military commanders or upon those who acted

Remember the rights of the savage, as we call him.

subject to their orders. But I am trying to point out the responsibility of the terrible consequences that follow upon such operations. Those hill tribes had committed no real offence against us. We, in the pursuit of our political objects, chose to establish military positions in their country. If they resisted, would not you have done the same? And when, going forth from their villages they had resisted, what you find is this, that those who went forth were slain, and that the village was burned. Again I say, have you considered the meaning of these words? The meaning of the burning of the village is, that the women and the children were driven forth to perish in the snows of winter. Is not that a terrible

The meaning of burning the village is, that the women and the children were driven forth to perish in the snows of winter.

supposition? Is not that a fact for such, I fear, it must be reckoned to be which does appeal to your hearts as women, which does lay a special hold and make a special claim upon your interest, which does rouse in you a sentiment of horror and grief, to think that the name of England, under no political necessity, but for a war as frivolous as ever was waged in the history of man, should be associated with consequences such as these?

... Remember the rights of the savage, as we call him. Remember that the happiness of his humble home, remember that the sanctity of life in the hill villages of Afghanistan among the winter snows, is as inviolable in the eye of Almighty God as can be your own. Remember that He who has united you together as human beings in the same flesh and blood, has bound you by the law of mutual love; that that mutual love is not limited by the shores of this island, is not limited by the boundaries of Christian civilisation; that it passes over the whole surface of the earth, and embraces the meanest along with the greatest in its unmeasured scope. And, therefore, I think that in appealing to you ungrudgingly to open your own feelings, and bear your own part in a political

> Our gallant troops have been called
> upon to ascend to an elevation of many thousand feet.

crisis like this, we are making no inappropriate demand, but are beseeching you to fulfil a duty which belongs to you, which, so far from involving any departure from your character as women, is associated with the fulfilment of that character, and the performance of its duties; the neglect of which would in future times be to you a source of pain and just mortification, and the fulfilment of which will serve to gild your own future years with sweet remembrances, and to warrant you in hoping that, each in your own place and sphere, you have raised your voice for justice, and have striven to mitigate the sorrows and misfortunes of mankind.

If I were a Glasgow man today
I would not be proud of it.

Henry George
1839–1897

'SCOTLAND AND SCOTSMEN' ADDRESS • CITY HALL • GLASGOW
18 FEBRUARY 1884

Henry George's fame in the Victorian era was derived from two books, *Our Land and Land Policy* (1870) and *Progress and Poverty* (1877), which attempted to explain the growing gap between the rich and the poor. 'It is true that wealth has been greatly increased, and that the average of comfort, leisure and refinement has been raised,' he wrote, 'but these gains are not general. In them the lowest class do not share.'[5]

He argued that this could only be remedied by replacing the various taxes levied on labour and capital with a single tax on the value of property. This radical voice from the Far West of America, although not ostentatiously socialist, led many British readers to socialism. 'Keir Hardie told me that it was *Progress and Poverty* which gave him his first ideas of socialism,' recalled Philip Snowden. 'No book ever written on the social problem made so many converts.'[6]

Henry George was an American writer, politician and political economist. He was the most influential proponent of the land value tax, also known as the 'single tax' on land, and inspired the economic ideology known as 'Georgism', the belief that everyone owned what he or she created, but that everything found in nature, most importantly land, belonged equally to all humanity.

George had been to Scotland before, but had seen 'nothing of the country'. His return visit, beginning in Dundee, did not go down well in the press. 'I have been accused of flattering Scotsmen,' he told his Glasgow audience. 'Now... I do not want to flatter anybody; and if Scotsmen don't like to be flattered, will you let me tell you tonight some home truths – some things, that are not complimentary?' That he proceeded to do, at some length.

I DRAW MY BLOOD from these islands. But it so happens this is the only place to which I can trace my ancestry with any certainty. I do not know but that some of my own kindred perhaps today live in Glasgow, and it is from Glasgow men and women some of my blood, at least, is drawn. I am not proud of it. If I were a Glasgow man today I would not be proud of it. Here you have a great and rich city, and here you have poverty and destitution that would appall a heathen. Right on these streets of yours the very stranger can see sights that could not be seen in any tribe of savages in anything like normal conditions.

'Let Glasgow flourish by the preaching of the word' – that is the motto of this great, proud city. What sort of a word is it that here has been preached? Or, let your preaching have been what it may, what is your practice? Are these the fruits of the word – this poverty, this destitution, this vice and degradation? To call this a Christian community is a slander on Christianity.

Low wages, want, vice, degradation – these are not the fruits of Christianity. They come from the ignoring and denial of the vital principles of Christianity. Let you people of Glasgow not merely erect church after church, you also subscribe money to send missionaries to the heathen. I wish the heathen were a little richer, that they might subscribe money and send missionaries to such so-called Christian communities as this – to point to the luxury, the very ostentation of wealth, on the one hand, and to the bare-footed, ill-clad women on the other; to your men and women with bodies stunted and minds distorted; to your little children growing up in such conditions that only a miracle can keep them pure!

Excuse me for calling your attention to these unpleasant truths; they are something that people with hearts in their breasts ought to think of... Now, consider what it implies – this crowding of men, women, and children together. People do not herd that way unless driven by dire want and necessity. These figures imply want and suffering, and brutish degradation, of which every citizen of Glasgow, every Scotsman, should be ashamed...

Scotland is relapsing into barbarism again... Will you, people who love Scotland, let it go on?

Why, in this great, rich city of yours, there are today numbers and numbers of men who cannot get employment. Here the wages of your engineers were reduced a little while ago, and they had to submit. The engineers of Belfast had also to submit to a reduction of wages, because there were so many unemployed shipwrights and engineers in Glasgow that they feared they could not maintain a strike. Am I not right in saying that such a state of things is but typical of that which exists everywhere throughout the civilised world? And I am bound to say that it is a state of things you ought to be ashamed of. I speak, not because they do not exist in my own country, for in their degree there is just the same state of things in America. But is not the spirit that, ignoring this, gives thanks and praise to the Almighty Father, cant of the worst kind?

... I have now seen something of Scotland, and let me tell you frankly that what I have seen does not raise my estimate of the Scottish character. Let me tell you frankly – seeing I have been accused of flattering you, and you say you can stand unpleasant truths, I have a good deal more respect for the Irish. The Irish have done some kicking against this infernal system, and you men in Scotland have got it yet to do.

The Scots are a logical people, as my friend says. I won't gainsay that; but their major premise must be a very curious one. I have really been wondering, since I have been in Scotland, whether you have not got things mixed a little. The Scots are a Bible-reading people. I have sometimes wondered whether, instead of reading 'In the beginning the Lord created the heavens and the earth' they haven't got 'In the beginning the lairds created the heavens and the earth.' Certainly the lairds have it all their own way through Scotland. Theirs is the land and all upon it; theirs is all that is beneath the land; theirs are the fishes in the rivers and in the lochs; theirs are the birds of the air; theirs are the salmon in the sea, even the seaweed that is thrown ashore, even the whales over a certain length, even the driftwood? Theirs are even the water and the air...

> ... I have now seen something of Scotland,
> and let me tell you frankly that what I have seen does not
> raise my estimate of the Scottish character.

What was Scotland made for? What was this earth made for? Was it not for humankind? ... Upon this land the curse that follows the expulsion of people is coming. People have been driven off the richest and best land, and the sites of their little homes and their little cultivated fields given up to sheep, and the sheep fattened. It was good grass where the people had been. That, everywhere, I learn, is giving way. I am told by capable authorities that where a thousand sheep 20 or 30 years ago could be kept, in places people had been driven off not 700 can be kept now.

There is a fungus moss creeping over the ground; Scotland is relapsing into barbarism again; even sheep are giving way to the solitude of the deer forest amid the grouse moor. Will you, people who love Scotland, let it go on?

Go in for what is your just and your natural right, the ownership of the land of Skye for its people.

Michael Davitt
1846–1906

SPEECH AT THE PORTREE HOTEL • ISLE OF SKYE

3 MAY 1887

On a sunny evening in the spring of 1887, the Irish republican politician and land reformer Michael Davitt arrived in Portree harbour on a steamer from the railway terminus at Strome. Accompanied by the local MP, Angus Sutherland, and JG MacKay, secretary of the Skye Land League, an 'immense' crowd escorted Davitt to his hotel bearing banners in Gaelic and English (which 'bore testimony to the strong desire for land reform and Home Rule', according to the *Freeman's Journal*) and preceded by pipers.

Michael Davitt was born at Straide, County Mayo, in 1846. Aged only six, he witnessed his family's eviction from their home and its destruction, which influenced his politics and interest in land reform. Raised in Lancashire, he later came to prominence as one of the founders of the Irish Land League and was often imprisoned for his outspoken speeches.

On reaching the Portree Hotel the enthusiastic crowd insisted upon a speech, which Davitt delivered from an upstairs window. The proliferation of large estates and absentee landlordism in the Highlands and Islands gave him a natural affinity with the area, while Davitt would have been aware that the Scottish campaign for land reform had resulted in legislation the previous year, the Crofters (Scotland) Act.

In 1879 Davitt had formed the Irish Land League, the techniques of which had been copied in Skye and across the region – the Highland Land League even consciously copied its name. This speech was from Davitt's second visit to Scotland, having first brought his message there in 1882.

I KNOW THAT THE sympathy you have shown by this enthusiastic welcome is extended more to the people I represent than to myself on account of anything that I have done personally. I am glad to know that recent distinguished visitors to your island have not succeeded in convincing you that the people of Ireland are wrong in their struggle for Home Rule. (Cheers.) I never believed for a moment that the people of this island, or of any part of the Highlands of Scotland, could be convinced by any amount of sophistry that the Irish cause was not a cause deserving of the sympathy of the Scottish people. (Cheers.)

Landlordism is ready to give up the ghost.

In many respects we are not only identical in race, but in political and social aspirations as well. The land system that has impoverished Ireland and made it the home of misery and agrarian crime has also been felt in this island and in other parts of Scotland. (Cheers.) I am sure the people of Skye are convinced that if the Irish succeed in abolishing landlordism an effective blow would be struck at the rest of a similar evil system in your island. (Cheers.)

Reading the mottos you have on your banners I find that you are a people who study the Bible. Well many of our modern philanthropists would rather you gave your spare time to the study of political economy. They think it was a mistake for the Creator to lay down a doctrine that the earth was created for the children of men. (Cheers.) They would rather call your attention to the study of Adam Smith and Malthus, writers who would try and make you believe that Providence made a

They would be better pleased if you agreed that your duty is to put up with misery and small patches of land.

mistake when the land was created for the people to live upon (Laughter and Cheers). They would rather you put the Bible on one side and took up the doctrines of those distinguished writers, and they would be better pleased if you agreed that your duty is to put up with misery and small patches of land in order that sheep and deer may enjoy the soil which God Almighty created for you.

I am not come as an apostle of that heartless creed of political economy. (Cheers.) I believe the land of Scotland, like the land of Ireland, was made by Providence to be enjoyed by the people, and I am not come here to advocate any half-hearted remedy (Cheers) for the grievances that exist in this island. I have come here to advise the people to follow our example in Ireland, to go in for the complete abolition of landlordism. (Cheers.) That system of legalised robbery is a social evil that must be got at in order to be torn up root and branch. This must be done before the misery, suffering, and degradation existent in Ireland can be cured, and my advice to the people of Portree and to the people of this island is

I am not come here to advocate any half-hearted remedy for the grievances that exist in this island.

not to be satisfied with half measures of change, but to go in for what is your just and your natural right to ownership of the land of Skye for its people. (Cheers.)

As for Ireland, I know well that in the coming struggle against the 87th Coercion Act of the century we will have the moral support of popular opinion in Scotland, and with that strength behind, and with the sympathy of the English and Welsh democracy as well, I hope the next time I come to Skye it will be my privilege to say that Home Rule has been won in Ireland, that landlordism is ready to give up the ghost. (Loud Cheers.)

Socialism proposes to dethrone the brute-god Mammon and to lift humanity into its place.

Keir Hardie
1856–1915

SPEECH ON THE 'SOCIALIST COMMONWEALTH' • HOUSE OF COMMONS

23 APRIL 1901

When Keir Hardie made his maiden speech in the House of Commons after winning West Ham South in 1892, there was an outcry. The press claimed he had worn a cap in the Chamber, although there is some evidence this was actually adorned by a Glasgow Member. Nevertheless, Hardie 'impressed the House with his earnestness, ability and courage'.[7] Even the Grand Old Man, William Gladstone, paid him the complement of his full attention.

The speech gained Hardie the undisputed leadership of the Independent Labour Party, but he also had a global role as chairman of the British section of the Socialist International. This speech, from another Commons debate nearly a decade later, reflects Hardie's internationalist outlook. We can only guess what Conservative, and even Liberal, MPs made of his vision of a 'Socialist Commonwealth' at the dawn of the Edwardian era.

(James) Keir Hardie (formerly James Kerr) was born in Lanarkshire in 1856, the illegitimate son of a farm servant. From the age of 11 he worked down the mines as a 'trapper', later progressing to trade unionism and, from 1887, socialism. Hardie moved to London in 1891 and was elected the 'independent Labour' MP for West Ham South the following year. He died from pneumonia in 1915.

I MAKE NO APOLOGY for bringing the question of Socialism before the House of Commons. It has long commanded the attention of the best minds in the country. It is a growing force in the thought of the world, and whether men agree or disagree with it, they have to reckon with it, and may as well begin by understanding it... and if it be argued that while that may be true of the Continent it is not true of this country, I reply that the facts and conditions now existing in this country are such as to make it extremely probable that the progress of Socialism in this country will be at a more rapid pace than in any other country in Europe...

While our population during the last century increased three and a half times, the wealth of the community increased over six times. But one factor in our national life remained with us all through the century, and is with us still, and that is that at the bottom of the social scale there is a mass of poverty and misery equal in magnitude to that which obtained 100 years ago. I submit that the true test of progress is not the accumulation of wealth in the hands of a few, but the

The pursuit of wealth corrupts the manhood of man.

elevation of a people as a whole. I admit frankly that a considerable improvement was made in the condition of the working people during the last century... but I respectfully submit to the House that there was more happiness, more comfort and more independence before machinery began to accumulate wealth...

During the last quarter of the century the condition of the working classes has been practically stationary. There have been slight increases of wages here and reductions of hours there, but the landlord with his increased rent has more than absorbed any advantage that may have been gained...

I come now to the causes which have forced thinking people of all ranks of society to reconsider their attitude towards socialism. I refer particularly to the great and alarming growth of what are known as trusts and syndicates in connection with industry... So long as industry is conducted by individuals competing one with another there is a chance of the article produced being supplied at an approximation to its market value, but competition has been found to be destructive of the interests of the owners and possessors of capital in this as in every other country. Three or four firms which formerly entered one market and competed with each other find it conducive to their interests to combine, thereby creating a monopoly which enables them to charge whatever price they like, and to treat their workpeople in any way that seems good to them...

Progress is not the accumulation of wealth in the hands of a few, but the elevation of a people as a whole.

We are rapidly approaching a point when the nation will be called upon to decide between an uncontrolled monopoly, conducted for the benefit and in the interests of its principal shareholders, and a monopoly owned, controlled, and manipulated by the State in the interests of the nation as a whole. I do not require to go far afield for arguments to support that part of my statement concerning the danger which the aggregation of wealth in a few hands is bringing upon us. This House and the British nation knows to their cost the danger which comes from allowing men to grow rich and permitting them to use their wealth to corrupt the press, to silence the pulpit, to degrade our national life, and to bring reproach and shame upon a great people, in order that a few unscrupulous scoundrels might be able to add to their ill-gotten gains...

Half a million of the people of this country benefit by the present system; the remaining millions of toilers and business men do not. The pursuit of wealth corrupts the manhood of men. We are called upon at the beginning of the 20th century to decide the question propounded in the Sermon on the Mount as to whether or not we will worship God or Mammon. The present day is a Mammon-worshipping age. Socialism proposes to dethrone the brute-god Mammon and to

> The British nation knows to their cost the danger which comes from allowing men to grow rich and permitting them to use their wealth to corrupt the press.

lift humanity into its place. I beg to submit in this very imperfect fashion the resolution on the Paper, merely premising that the last has not been heard of the Socialist movement either in the country or on the floor of this House, but that, just as sure as Radicalism democratised the system of Government politically in the last century so will Socialism democratise the country industrially during the century upon which we have just entered. I beg to move.

When is a war not a war?
When it is carried on by methods of barbarism in South Africa.

Sir Henry Campbell-Bannerman
1836–1908

'METHODS OF BARBARISM' SPEECH TO
NATIONAL REFORM UNION • LONDON

14 JUNE 1901

The South African, or Boer, War divided Liberals at the turn of the last century, polarising the party between Imperialists and those who regarded the conflict as morally reprehensible. In 1901 the UK government assumed the war was all but won, but when the Boers adopted guerrilla tactics the British Army responded by burning their farms and interning Boer families in what became known as concentration camps.

Sir Henry Campbell-Bannerman was born in Glasgow in 1836. Educated at Glasgow High School and, after travelling in Europe for a year, the Universities of Glasgow and Cambridge, he worked for his family firm before entering Parliament in 1868 as the MP for Stirling Burghs. Campbell-Bannerman held office as Chief Secretary for Ireland and War Secretary before becoming Liberal leader and Prime Minister from 1905. He died in office three years later.

'CB', as he was known, had been deeply affected by the account given to him by Emily Hobhouse, who had visited camps containing 60,000 Boer women and children. Rising to speak at a dinner in London given by the National Reform Union, CB could not contain his anger, and railed against the 'methods of barbarism' being directed against the Boers. A journalist noted the 'strong suppressed emotion' from which CB was evidently 'suffering', observing that, unusually for him, he spoke without notes.

Once the press picked up on the speech, CB was accused of betraying the army, a crime made all the worse by his being a former War Secretary, even though he took care to praise the armed forces, just as critics of the Iraq War did a century later. CB's speech provoked praise and derision in equal measure, while no fewer than 50 Liberal Imperialist MPs later walked out of the Commons, refusing to support a motion condemning the camps.

WE CANNOT DISGUISE from ourselves that at every gathering there is present the spectre of this terrible war ('Hear, hear'). What would not all of our countrymen give, whatever party they belong to, if we could be free from the fear and misgivings and the horrors associated with this war? I have been taken to task, and some writers in the Unionist press have used great acerbity of language, because the other day I said that there could only be an insignificant fraction of the Liberal Party who approved the policy – as I said, the unwise and unworthy policy (Cheers) – of pressing unconditional surrender on those who are opposing us in this war.

I have been called upon to produce a single Liberal anywhere who has approved that policy. What is that policy? That now that we have got the men we have been fighting against down, we should punish them as severely as possible, devastate their country, burn their homes, break up their very instruments of agriculture, and destroy the machinery by which food is produced. ('Shame.') It is that we should sweep – as the Spaniards did in Cuba; and how we denounced the Spaniards – the women and children into camps in which they are destitute of all the decencies and comforts, and many of the necessities of life, and in some of which the death-rate has risen so high as 430 in the 1,000 ('Shame.')

I do not say for a moment, because I do not think for a moment, that this is an intentional policy of His Majesty's Government, but it is the policy of the writers

We cannot disguise from ourselves that at every gathering there is present the spectre of this terrible war.

in the press who support them; and, at all events, it is the thing which is being done at this moment in the name and by the authority of this most humane and Christian nation ('Shame'). Yesterday I asked the Leader of the House of Commons when the information would be afforded, of which we are so sadly in want. My request was refused. Mr Balfour treated us with a short disquisition on the nature of the war. (Laughter.) A phrase often used was that 'war is war', but when one comes to ask about it, one is told that no war is going on – that it is not war. (Laughter.) When is a war not a war? When it is carried on by methods of barbarism in South Africa (Cheers)... Do you think that we can be intimidated today by being taunted as Little Englanders and pro-Boers?... Let us disregard all this nonsense. Little Englanders! Well, Sir, I was born a good many years ago. I was born a citizen of a great England – an England that has grown greater still. It has grown in a century of almost unbroken peace. It has grown mainly under the principles and under the conduct of the Liberal Party. (Cheers.) It has grown, and I hope it will grow greater still if the Liberal Party never desert their name and never abandon their faith (Cheers.)...

With reference to this war, I regard it as the greatest disaster which in modern times has befallen the British nation, both in its conduct and in what I fear must be its consequences. I am not going tonight elaborately into the causes of the war. But this must be said with confidence, that the war has arisen from the alienation of two races. Up to a few years ago, a satisfactory progress. The two peoples were living in absolute cordiality and friendship. There had been no doubt in the Transvaal friction in minor matters, but nothing that would have led to any collision. (Cheers.) Suddenly there was perpetrated the crime that has

> They have saved us; they have repaired the blunders, and have enabled us to face the disasters of this war.

been the root of the whole mischief, a subsidised insurrection. (Cheers.) And an armed invasion of the South African Republic organised by the prime minister of the Cape Colony, a privy counselor of the queen, with his confederates the gold gamblers of the Rand (Cheers). A conspiracy conducted with every circumstance of falsehood. It was the manner – I say it with shame and regret – in which that infamous transaction was regarded and treated by the people here and in South Africa – they were made the heroes of the British party as it was called – which shook to its foundation the confidence of the Dutch people in the good faith of this country. That is the origin of the war. (Cheers.)

Now, gentlemen, in my opinion, you have no right to forget or disregard that circumstance when you are dealing with the question of the hostility of the Boers... I do not propose to enter either tonight upon the question of the conduct of the war. The valour of our soldiers and the fortitude of our people we all recognise. ('Hear, Hear.') They have saved us; they have repaired the blunders, and have enabled us to face the disasters of this war.

We are willing, as we have always been, to do our bit, but we object to slavery.

David Kirkwood
1872–1955

SPEECH TO MUNITIONS WORKERS • PARKHEAD WORKS • GLASGOW

DECEMBER 1915

One of the original Red Clydesiders, by 1910 David Kirkwood was playing a leading part in trade union activism. In 1915 he led an agitation to gain the Clyde engineers an increase of 2*d* an hour, but quickly accepted the compromise offer of 1*d*, so as not to affect the war effort. The restrictions of the Munitions Act were a major bone of contention, while discontent among engineers was also growing because of the widespread raising of house rents.

David Kirkwood was born at Parkhead, Glasgow, and was active in the industrial politics of the area for the next half century. In 1922 he was elected MP for Dumbarton Burghs and was twice suspended from Parliament. In 1951 he was elevated to the House of Lords. His biography, My Life of Revolt, was published in 1935.

Property owners were using shortage of accommodation for munition workers to push up prices, and there were also dramatic instances of soldiers' wives being evicted for inability to pay. Kirkwood became heavily involved in these protests. Although he always denied urging a strike of munition workers, when speeches opposing the Munitions Act were banned, including one he had written for a meeting at Glasgow City Halls, Kirkwood arranged a meeting at Parkhead Works, and delivered the speech he had prepared.

As this was the first big speech I had ever made,' he recalled in his memoirs, 'I took great pains with it. I still think it is about the best speech I ever made. It came out of my mouth like shells from a gun.'[8] A few months later, Kirkwood was deported to Edinburgh as a trouble maker under the Defence of the Realm Act. He remained there for 14 months, consistently refusing to sign any document promising 'good behaviour' as a condition of his return to the Clyde. The Times, not unreasonably, described him as a 'fiery man'.[9]

Fellow-engineers, the country is at war. The country must win. In order to win, we must throw our whole soul into the production of munitions. Now we come to the point of difference. The Government and its supporters think that to get the best out of us, they must take away our liberty. So we are deprived of the chief thing that distinguishes free men from slaves, the right to leave a master when we wish to. If I work in Beardmore's I am as much his property as

The Government and its supporters think that to get the best out of us, they must take away our liberty.

if he had branded a 'B' on my brow... They have us and they know it. Mr Lloyd George claims that all this is necessary in order to win the War. It is a strange doctrine. It amounts to this, that slaves are better than free men. I deny it. I maintain that for peace or war free men are better than slaves... We are willing, as we have always been, to do our bit, but we object to slavery.

I am not here, then, as the accused; I am here as the accuser of capitalism dripping with blood from head to foot.

John Maclean
1879–1923

SPEECH FROM THE DOCK · HIGH COURT · EDINBURGH

9 MAY 1918

Encouraged by the success of the Bolshevik Revolution, by 1917 John Maclean was advocating a revolutionary solution to the Great War, and called upon British workers to emulate the Bolsheviks' recent success. But his growing prestige as a revolutionary socialist (he was appointed the Soviet consul in Glasgow) also drew him to the attention of the British authorities.

In February 1918, when the German army was mounting its last big offensive of the war, the general officer commanding the army in Scotland argued that action be taken against Maclean, and on 15 April he was arrested for sedition, mainly for calling on workers to deliver a revolutionary blow on May Day.

Maclean's arrest meant he was absent from those demonstrations in Glasgow, but he used his trial as a platform for an impassioned denunciation of the war. The speech soon entered left-wing folklore, and it's easy to see why. When the Lord Justice General said at the end of Maclean's oration that he be 'sent to penal servitude for a period of five years', Maclean turned to his comrades in the court and urged: 'Keep it going, boys; keep it going.'

John Maclean was born in Pollokshaws, Glasgow, in 1879, the son of a potter and weaver. Raised by his mother, he qualified as a teacher in 1900, and worked as such until he was dismissed on account of his political activities during the First World War. Thereafter Maclean devoted himself to revolutionary socialism. He died, penniless, in 1923.

IT HAS BEEN SAID that they cannot fathom my motive. For the full period of my active life I have been a teacher of economics to the working classes, and my contention has always been that capitalism is rotten to its foundations, and must give place to a new society. I had a lecture, the principal heading of which was 'Thou shalt not steal; thou shalt not kill', and I pointed out that as a consequence of the robbery that goes on in all civilised countries today, our respective countries have had to keep armies, and that inevitably our armies must clash together. On that and on other grounds, I consider capitalism the most infamous, bloody and evil system that mankind has ever witnessed. My language is regarded as extravagant language, but the events of the past four years have proved my contention...

I am out for the benefit of society, not for any individual human being, but I realise this, that justice and freedom can only be obtained when society is placed on a sound economic basis. That sound economic basis is wanting today, and hence the bloodshed we are having. I have not tried to get young men particularly. The young men have come to my meetings as well as the old men. I know quite well that in the reconstruction of society, the class interests of

No government is going to take from me my right to speak, my right to protest against wrong.

those who are on top will resist the change, and the only factor in society that can make for a clean sweep in society is the working class. Hence the class war. The whole history of society has proved that society moves forward as a consequence of an under-class overcoming the resistance of a class on top of them. So much for that.

I also wish to point out to you this, that when the late King Edward VII died, I took as the subject of one of my lectures 'Edward the Peacemaker'. I pointed out at the time that his *entente cordiale* with France and his alliance with Russia were for the purpose of encircling Germany as a result of the coming friction between Germany and this country because of commercial rivalry. I then denounced that title 'Edward the Peacemaker' and said that it should be 'Edward the Warmaker'. The events which have ensued prove my contention right up to the hilt, I am only proceeding along the lines upon which I have proceeded for many years. I have pointed out at my economic classes that, owing to the surplus created by the workers, it was necessary to create a market outside this country, because of the inability of the workers to purchase the wealth they create. You must have markets abroad, and in order to have these markets you must have empire. I have also pointed out that the capitalist development of Germany since the Franco-Prussian War has forced upon that country the necessity for empire as well as

What is moral for the one class is absolutely immoral for the other and vice versa.

this country, and in its search for empire there must be a clash between these two countries. I have been teaching that and what I have taught is coming perfectly true.

I wish no harm to any human being, but I, as one man, am going to exercise my freedom of speech. No human being on the face of the earth, no government is going to take from me my right to speak, my right to protest against wrong, my right to do everything that is for the benefit of mankind. I am not here, then, as the accused; I am here as the accuser of capitalism dripping with blood from head to foot...

I have taken up unconstitutional action at this time because of the abnormal circumstances and because precedent has been given by the British government. I am a socialist, and have been fighting and will fight for an absolute reconstruction of society for the benefit of all. I am proud of my conduct. I have squared my conduct with my intellect, and if everyone had done so this war

> My contention has always been that capitalism is rotten to its foundations.

would not have taken place. I act square and clean for my principles. I have nothing to retract. I have nothing to be ashamed of. Your class position is against my class position. There are two classes of morality. There is the working class morality and there is the capitalist class morality. There is this antagonism as there is the antagonism between Germany and Britain. A victory for Germany is a defeat for Britain; a victory for Britain is a defeat for Germany. And it is exactly the same so far as our classes are concerned. What is moral for the one class is absolutely immoral for the other, and vice-versa. No matter what your accusations against me may be, no matter what reservations you keep at the back of your head, my appeal is to the working class. I appeal exclusively to them because they and they only can bring about the time when the whole world will be in one brotherhood, on a sound economic foundation. That, and that alone, can be the means of bringing about a re-organisation of society. That can only be obtained when the people of the world get the world, and retain the world.

Courage is the thing.
All goes if courage goes.

JM Barrie
1860–1937

RECTORIAL ADDRESS • UNIVERSITY OF ST ANDREWS

3 MAY 1922

The playwright JM Barrie was elected Rector of St Andrews University in 1919 but postponed his installation for two years. This address, therefore, was delivered towards the end of his three-year term. He spent many months working on his speech, and firmly in mind was the fact that many of the students he would be addressing would have experienced the horrors of the Great War.

'As the date of Barrie's address grew nearer,' wrote one of Barrie's biographers, 'he wrote, revised, obsessively rewrote, and with each day grew still more anxious.'[10] By the time he arrived at St Andrews he was exhausted through lack of sleep and strained nerves, and even made final changes on the morning of his address. At first he could not speak, then when he did his voice was inaudible and he nervously fiddled with a paper knife lying on the table before him. Suddenly a voice called out: 'Put it down, Jamie, you'll cut your throat.'

Sir James Matthew Barrie was born in 1860 at a small house in Kirriemuir, the son of a weaver. Later, a succession of books – most famously **Peter Pan** *– and long-running theatrical productions brought him great wealth, critical acclaim and honours. But Barrie's private life was troubled and he died in 1937.*

This broke the ice, and as the laughter died down Barrie 'began to work that other magic once more. In a voice now become firm and clear he soon held his audience in rapt attention, and, launching into confessional mode, he confided in them apparently some of his innermost thoughts and fears.' Barrie did this via McConnachie, a fictional public projection of his many selves. After nearly an hour and a half he sat down. For a moment the hall was silent, then, all rising to their feet, the students burst into thunderous applause. Newspapers carried columns of praise, and Barrie's publishers quickly published the speech with the simple title 'Courage'.

BEWARE YOUR BETTERS bringing presents. What is wanted is something run by yourselves. You have more in common with the Youth of other lands than Youth and Age can ever have with each other; even the hostile countries sent out many a son very like ours, from the same sort of homes, the same sort of universities, who had as little to do as our youth had with the origin of the great adventure. Can we doubt that many of these on both sides who have gone over and were once opponents are now friends? You ought to have a League of Youth of all countries as your beginning, ready to say to all Governments, 'We will fight each other but only when we are sure of the necessity.' Are you equal to your job, you young men? If not, I call upon the red-gowned women to lead the way. I sound to myself as if I were advocating a rebellion, though I am really asking for a larger friendship. Perhaps I may be arrested on leaving the hall. In such a cause I should think that I had at last proved myself worthy to be your Rector.

We will fight each other, but only when we are sure of the necessity.

You will have to work harder than ever, but possibly not so much at the same things; more at modern languages certainly if you are to discuss that League of Youth with the students of other nations when they come over to St Andrews for the Conference. I am far from taking a side against the classics. I should as soon argue against your having tops to your heads; that way lie the best tops. Science, too, has at last come to its own in St Andrews. It is the surest means of teaching you how to know what you mean when you say. So you will have to work harder. Isaak Walton quotes the saying that doubtless the Almighty could have created a finer fruit than the strawberry, but that doubtless also He never did. Doubtless also He could have provided us with better fun than hard work, but I don't know what it is. To be born poor is probably the next best thing. The greatest glory that has ever come to me was to be swallowed up in London, not knowing a soul, with no means of subsistence, and the fun of working till the stars went out. To have known any one would have spoilt it...

You will all fall into one of those two callings, the joyous or the uncongenial; and one wishes you into the first, though our sympathy, our esteem, must go rather to the less fortunate, the braver ones who 'turn their necessity to glorious gain' after they have put away their dreams. To the others will go the easy prizes of life, success, which has become a somewhat odious onion nowadays, chiefly because we so often give the name to the wrong thing. When you reach the evening of your days you will, I think, see – with, I hope, becoming cheerfulness – that we are all failures, at least all the best of us...

This courage is proof of our immortality.

Courage is the thing. All goes if courage goes. What says our glorious Johnson of courage: 'Unless a man has that virtue he has no security for preserving any other.' We should thank our Creator three times daily for courage instead of for our bread, which, if we work, is surely the one thing we have a right to claim of Him. This courage is a proof of our immortality, greater even than gardens 'when the eve is cool.' Pray for it...

Another piece of advice; almost my last. For reasons you may guess I must give this in a low voice. Beware of McConnachie. When I look in a mirror now it is his face I see. I speak with his voice. I once had a voice of my own, but nowadays I hear it from far away only, a melancholy, lonely, lost little pipe. I wanted to be an explorer, but he willed otherwise. You will all have your McConnachies luring you off the high road. Unless you are constantly on the watch, you will

> *We should thank our Creator three times daily*
> *for courage instead of our bread.*

find that he has slowly pushed you out of yourself and taken your place. He has rather done for me. I think in his youth he must somehow have guessed the future and been fleggit by it, flichtered from the nest like a bird, and so our eggs were left, cold. He has clung to me, less from mischief than for companionship; I half like him and his penny whistle; with all his faults he is as Scotch as peat; he whispered to me just now that you elected him, not me, as your Rector.

I shall vote...
in favour of our going into the election
as a Party fighting to win.

Andrew Bonar Law
1858–1923

SPEECH TO CONSERVATIVE MPS • CARLTON CLUB • LONDON

19 OCTOBER 1922

By the beginning of October 1922 many Conservatives, both in Parliament and beyond, had become bitterly hostile towards the Liberal/Conservative coalition headed up by the charismatic Welshman David Lloyd George. The Prime Minister's aggressive stance on Graeco–Turkish relations, raising the prospect of another conflict, forced Andrew Bonar Law's hand, and he warned in a letter to the *Daily Express* that Britain could not 'act alone as the policeman of the world'.

This intervention attracted support from a number of Tory MPs, who urged Bonar Law to reassume the party leadership. Bonar Law did not respond immediately, hesitant about openly challenging the government. The predominant issue at that time, however, was whether the Conservatives should reassert their political independence – in other words quit the coalition. Matters came to a head at a meeting of Conservative ministers and MPs held at the Carlton Club on 19 October 1922.

Andrew Bonar Law was born in New Brunswick, Canada, to the Rev James Law, an Ulsterman of Scottish descent. The only Prime Minister to have been born outside the British Isles, he was also the shortest serving of the 20th century, inhabiting 10 Downing Street for just 211 days. A businessman before entering Parliament, Bonar Law made his political reputation opposing Home Rule for Ireland, and in particular for Ulster.

Austen Chamberlain, Bonar Law's successor as party leader, argued that the best interests of the party were served by continuing the coalition, and Bonar Law only decided the day before that he would speak against. One observed reckoned Bonar Law looked 'ill', his 'voice so weak that people quite close to him had to strain their ears – but his manner was clear and distinctly put'. The result of Law's 15-minute speech was unequivocal. The question was called, ballot cards distributed and counted: 187 MPs supported the motion, 88 opposed it, with one abstention. There was no doubt 'that all had turned on Bonar Law's intervention', not least the immediate resignations of Lloyd George and Chamberlain.

I CONFESS FRANKLY, that in the immediate crisis in front of us I do personally attach more importance to keeping our Party a united body than to winning the next election.

The feeling against the continuation of the Coalition is so strong that if we follow Austen Chamberlain's advice our Party will be broken and a new party will be formed; and not the worst of the evils of that is this, that on account of those who have gone, who are supposed to be the more moderate men, what is left of the Conservative Party will become more reactionary, and I, for one, say that though what you call the reactionary element in our party has always been there and must always be there, if it is the sole element, our party is absolutely lost.

I do personally attach more importance to keeping our Party a united body, then to winning the next election.

Therefore if you agree with Mr Chamberlain in this crisis I will tell you what I think will be the result. It will be a repetition of what happened after Peel passed the Corn Bill. The body that is cast off will slowly become the Conservative Party, but it will take a generation before it gets back to the influence which the Party ought to have... [but] the great bulk of our supporters would say they refuse to leave their organisation, and would continue as members of the Unionist Party.

That is the position... I shall vote – and for the reason that it is the best chance of keeping our Party as an integral Party – in favour of our going into the election as a Party fighting to win...

This is a question in regard to which our system (and a good system it has been) has hitherto gone on this principle: that the Party elects a leader, and that the leader chooses the policy, and if the Party does not like it, they have to get another leader.

*The world continues to offer glittering prizes
to those who have stout hearts
and sharp swords.*

Lord Birkenhead
1872–1930

RECTORIAL ADDRESS • UNIVERSITY OF GLASGOW

7 NOVEMBER 1923

FE Smith, or Lord Birkenhead as he latterly became, did not lack self-confidence. Aged ten, he announced to schoolmates his intention of becoming Lord Chancellor. That he did in 1919, while his steady progression through the peerage, from Baron (1919) to Viscount (1921) and Earl (1922) 'only swelled his self-importance'.[11]

Since the First World War Birkenhead's views had become progressively more reactionary. He was alarmed by the threat of Bolshevism and supported Lloyd George's attempt to merge his coalition Liberals with the Conservatives into a single anti-Labour Party. When that failed he argued that the coalition must continue indefinitely, a view not shared by the majority of Tory MPs who voted to quit the coalition at the Carlton Club in October 1922.

FE Smith, Lord Birkenhead, was born in Birkenhead in 1872, the son of an estate agent/barrister. He shone at Oxford and won the working-class constituency of Walton at the 1906 general election. In 1915 Smith became solicitor general, then attorney general and, in 1919, Lord Chancellor. He played a key role in reaching a settlement with Ireland in 1921 and died in 1930.

Out of office, Birkenhead gave greater vent to his reactionary instincts, and this Rectorial address to students at the University of Glasgow in November 1923 achieved notoriety beyond that city. Although the recent war dictated that most politicians paid lip service to the League of Nations, Birkenhead opted instead to invoke his 'his neo-Darwinian view of international conflict'. As a result, the former Lord Chancellor (and future Secretary of State for India) was denounced from pulpits and pacifist platforms up and down the country.

FROM THE VERY dawn of the world man has been a combative animal. To begin with, he fought violently for his own elemental needs; later, perhaps in tribal or communal quarrel; later still, with the growth of greater communities, upon a larger and more sophisticated scale. And it is to be specially noted that there have nevertheless almost always existed men who sincerely but very foolishly believed; firstly, that no war would arise in their own day; and, secondly (when that war did arise), that for some reason or other it would be the last. At this point the idealist degenerates into the pacifist; and it is at this point consequently that he becomes a danger to the community of which he is citizen...

Everybody recognizes that war is both cruel and hateful. But is it even conceivable that it can ever be abolished?

A broader consideration must now in its turn be examined. We are told that the object aimed at is the abolition of war. Everybody recognises that war is both cruel and hateful. But is it even conceivable that it can ever be abolished? Is the ownership of the world to be stereotyped by perpetual tenure in the hands of those who possess its different territories today? If it is, very strange and undesirable consequences will one day follow. For nations wax and wane, so that a power competent in one age to govern an empire, perhaps remote, in the general interest of the world, will in another abuse a dominion for which it no longer possesses the necessary degree of vigour...

And the general extrusion of savage races from regions, for instance, the American continent, and certain of the South Sea islands, to which they had some considerable legal right, shows that, rightly or wrongly, nations of stronger fibre, confronted by indigenous weaklings, have always asserted the right of forcible expropriation. No one (to make the argument short) who has studied the history of the world has ever defended the view that the supreme interest of evolutionary humanity can support a definitive delimination for all time of the surface of the world.

But if such a final distribution is impracticable and even undesirable, by what agency are modifications to be made? Voluntary cessations of territory have not been frequent in the past; and there seems little reason to suppose that they will become more fashionable in the future. For many thousands of years the emergence of new and martial nations has been gradually marked by violent readjustments of national boundaries. It may, of course, be the case that human nature has so completely altered that some new method is discoverable. I confess, however, that none has up to the present occurred to my own mind.

From the very dawn of the world man has been a combatitive animal.

It may, perhaps, be charged against those who sincerely hold the views which I have attempted to make plain, that we carry in our veins the virus which coloured the sombre and unmoral genius of Treitschke, and which found popular expression in the mosquito propaganda of von Bernhardi. But such a charge, if made, would be patently unjust. We neither hold nor have we preached these doctrines. We diagnose certain diseases. We did not create them. A distinction must surely be drawn between him who calls attention to the risk of conflagration and that other who puts his torch to inflammable material.

> A distinction must surely be drawn between him who calls attention to the risk of conflagration and that other who puts his torch to inflammable material.

The purpose and moral of these general observations may be summarised in a few concluding observations. For as long a time as the records of history have been preserved human societies passed through a ceaseless process of evolution and adjustment. This process has sometimes been pacific, but more often it has resulted from warlike disturbance. The strength of different nations, measured in terms of arms, varies from century to century. The world continues to offer glittering prizes to those who have stout hearts and sharp swords; it is therefore extremely improbable that the experience of future ages will differ in any material respect from that which has happened since the twilight of the human race. It is for us, therefore, who in our history have proved ourselves a martial, rather than a military, people to abstain, as has been our habit, from provocation; but to maintain in our own hand the adequate means for our own protection; and, so equipped, to march with heads erect and bright eyes along the road of our imperial destiny.

Why will we take office?
Because we are to shirk no responsibility
that comes to us in the course of the
evolution of our Movement.

Ramsay MacDonald
1866–1937

SPEECH AT DEMONSTRATION • ROYAL ALBERT HALL • LONDON
8 JANUARY 1924

Ramsay MacDonald's place in history is secure as the first Labour Prime Minister of the United Kingdom. His aim as Leader of the Opposition had always been to push the Liberals aside and establish Labour as the permanent alternative to the Conservatives in a newly aligned two-party system. This strategy paid off earlier than he expected.

In November 1923 the fledgling Conservative premier Stanley Baldwin called a surprise general election, feeling himself bound by a pledge made by his predecessor, Andrew Bonar Law, that tariff reform could not take place without the country's consent. Baldwin lost, but with 259 seats to Labour's 191 and the Liberals' 159, the situation was in flux. When Asquith, the Liberal leader, made it clear he would neither support the Conservatives nor coalesce with Labour, the path was clear for a minority Labour administration.

James Ramsay MacDonald was born in 1866 in a 'but-'n'-ben' cottage in the small fishing port of Lossiemouth, the illegitimate son of two farm workers. He became leader of the Labour Party in 1911 and Prime Minister for the first time in 1924. MacDonald led another minority government from 1929–31 and then headed a National Government including Conservatives and Liberals, a compromise that earned the moniker the 'great betrayal' and infamy within the Labour ranks. He died in 1937.

Early in January 1924, MacDonald returned to London from his native Lossiemouth. Parliament met on 8 January and that evening he addressed a great demonstration at the Albert Hall. (The King later complained to MacDonald about the singing of the 'Red Flag' and the 'Marseillaise'.) 'With characteristic skill, he managed at one and the same time to tap the vein of emotional, utopian socialism which played such a large part in the Labour movement,' wrote MacDonald's biographer David Marquand, 'and yet to make it clear that the Labour Party would take office in a severely pragmatic spirit.'[12] When Baldwin presented a King's Speech and lost the vote on the Address, he left office on 22 January and MacDonald kissed hands as the new Prime Minister.

I THINK IT IS perfectly proper to describe this as a great victory demonstration. We have been in battle, we have brought back the trophies. We went away 144 strong, we came back 192, and amongst the 192 I am very glad and very proud to say we have three women. We have four million and a half electors standing solidly behind us in the country. A very good beginning, not an ending by any means. Today a new world seems to be opening out before us, and we cannot help thinking of the old one...

A sudden change has come upon our outlook. We are on the threshold of Government. We may be called upon within the next few days to take upon our shoulders the responsibility of office. We shall do it. Why? Not because we want it. Has any heir been so foolish as to hasten off the stage of this mortal life a father of his who is going to hand him over a bankrupt state? If there be such an [sic] one he is not to be found in the Labour Party.

> Today a new world seems to be opening out before us,
> and we cannot help thinking of the old one...

Why will we take office? Because we are to shirk no responsibility that comes to us in the course of the evolution of our Movement. There are risks, certainly, risks on every side – risks behind, before us, to the right of us, and to the left of us. Ah, but there is more than risks, there is a call. We have built our final habitations away on the horizon. We are a party of idealists. We are a party that away in the dreamland of imagination dwells in the social organisation fairer and more perfect than any organization that mankind has ever know. That is true, but we are not going to jump there. We are going to walk there. We are upon a pilgrimage, we are on a journey. One step enough for me. One step. Yes, on one condition – that it leads to a next step. If we shirked our responsibilities now we ourselves would be inflicting upon ourselves the defeat that our enemies could not inflict upon us. So we accept our responsibilities...

As I say, I am not thinking of Party. I am thinking of national wellbeing. I want a Labour Government to repair the damage that has been done since

> We are a party that away in the dreamland
> of imagination dwells in the social organisation fairer
> and more perfect than any organisation.

1914 to the homes, minds, the education, and the politics of our people. I want to encourage promising growths, making for peace, for happiness, and for contentment in the world. Human beings cannot be content whilst they are suffering injustice, and the man who declares for contentment declares for everything. He knows what he means.

I want a Labour Government, so that the life of the nation may be carried on. Nineteen twenty-four is not the last in God's programme of creation. My friends, we will be dead and gone and forgotten and generation after generation will come, and there will still be the search for the Holy Grail by knights like Keir Hardie. The shield of love and the spear of justice will still be in the hands of good and upright men and women, and the ideal of a great future will still be in front of our people. I see no end, thank God, to these things. I see my horizon, I see my own skyline, but I am convinced that when my children or children's children get there there will be another skyline, another horizon, another dawning, another glorious beckoning from heaven itself. That is my faith, and in that faith I go on and my colleagues go on, doing in their own lives what they can to make their addition, to contribute something substantial to the well-being, the happiness and the holiness of human life.

Save the country
from a Government which...
I think the country has conclusively shown
in the recent election it does not want.

Duchess of Atholl
1874–1960

MAIDEN SPEECH • HOUSE OF COMMONS

18 JANUARY 1924

Despite the Duchess of Atholl's Conservative affiliation, it was actually the Liberal Prime Minister, David Lloyd George, who first suggested that she stand for Parliament. King George V, however, tried to discourage her, warning that politics would distract from her domestic commitments. Happily, she felt able to leave such duties to her husband, himself a former MP, and he also urged her to stand, helping her practice public speaking.

As a former opponent of women's suffrage, the Duchess was an unusual prospect as Scotland's first female MP, but she believed that by putting herself forward as a candidate she would help Conservative men become accustomed to women in politics. At the general election of 1923 she was narrowly elected MP for Kinross and West Perthshire, her husband's former constituency. Nationally, the Labour Party increased its representation and soon formed a minority administration, the first time the UK had had a 'Socialist' government.

Katharine Marjory Stewart-Murray was born in Edinburgh, the eldest of the five children of Sir James Henry Ramsay, 10th baronet. She studied composition at the Royal College of Music under Sir Hubert Parry, hoping initially for a career as a pianist or composer. Instead, she returned to Scotland and devoted herself to public service. She became Duchess of Atholl on her husband's succession to the title of the 8th Duke of Atholl in 1917.

The Duchess was extremely nervous before her maiden speech, and stayed up rehearsing for most of the previous night. Once on her feet she found sufficient confidence and made what was judged to be a brilliant speech, ranging over a number of topics (including the Church of Scotland and juvenile unemployment centres) and ending with the rejoinder that the country did not actually want a Labour government, which is the section reproduced here. One newspaper hailed her speech as 'the sensation of the debate'.[13]

THE LEADER OF THE Opposition [Stanley Baldwin], in his speech on
Tuesday, levelled the criticism at the Gracious Speech that it was a
miscellaneous collection of odds and ends. There are always two ways of
describing a thing. Another way in which to describe it, I think, would be to say
that it is a very comprehensive Speech – a Speech which shows understanding of
the needs of many and varying sections of our people. It proposes to give effect to
the arrangements concluded with the Dominion Prime Ministers at the Imperial
Conference; to stimulate employment by various means of tried value; and to
endeavour to obtain an agreed and settled policy with regard to agriculture.
It also proposes various measures of social reform, on most of which, I think,
there has been general agreement between parties.

> *To bring in a Government…*
> *that it is to be given a blank cheque,*
> *at least will come into office with a blank programme.*

It seems to me, if I may say so, that Liberal Members incur a great responsibility
if they refuse to support a comprehensive, non-contentious programme of the
kind that has been put forward, in order to bring in a Government which, though
it may be denied by the right hon Member for Paisley [Mr Asquith] and his
followers that it is to be given a blank cheque, at least will come into office with a
blank programme, as to which the Leader of the Opposition has given no indication
even at the 11th hour. If even 50 Liberal Members – elected, as I believe a good
many were, at the last Election, by Conservative votes, or elected on the slogan of
'Vote Liberal and keep the Socialists out,' as I understand some of these gentlemen were – be true to their election pledges, they will save their party the odium
of incurring this great responsibility, and save the country from a Government
which, with all due respect to hon Members who may compose it, I think the
country has conclusively shown in the recent election it does not want.

The bricklayer and the bricklayers' labourers cannot afford to purchase houses which the bricklayer and the bricklayers' labourers are building.

John Wheatley
1869–1930

SPEECH DURING DEBATE ON HOUSING (FINANCIAL PROVISIONS) BILL,
HOUSE OF COMMONS

23 JUNE 1924

John Wheatley remains one of the outstanding figures in early Labour politics. A devout Catholic, he moved from the coalmines to municipal politics, and finally to the House of Commons in 1922. His formidable debating skills ensured him a place in the first minority Labour government formed by Ramsay MacDonald in January 1924. Wheatley was appointed Minister of Health, then a wide-ranging brief which included public housing.

John Wheatley was born in 1869 in Bonmahon, County Waterford, the son of a labourer. In 1876 the family left for Scotland and Wheatley grew up in Lanarkshire. Wheatley joined his father as a miner aged 11 and worked underground for more than 12 years. After a decade as a councillor, Wheatley was elected the MP for Shettleston in 1922, holding the seat until his death eight years later.

Wheatley's Housing (Financial Provisions) Act – known colloquially as the 'Wheatley Act' – was the only major legislative achievement of that short-lived 1924 Labour government. Until its provisions for subsidy were repealed by the National Government in 1934, a substantial proportion of all rented local authority housing in Britain was built under its terms and 60 years later there were still people in Scotland who spoke of 'Wheatley houses'. Bringing together trade unions, building firms and local authorities, the Act guaranteed central government funding provided that building standards laid out in the legislation were adhered to.

The Act, however, did little for slum clearance, although it sealed Wheatley's reputation despite the loss of another measure, the Building Materials Bill, which would have given central government a wide range of controls over supplies of building materials to local councils operating the Housing Act. This speech is from the Second Reading of the successful Bill, during which he makes the philosophical case for an increased subsidy.

THE QUESTION IS put to me in the press and in public, 'Why pay £9 for 40 years when you can get for a £6 subsidy for 20 years all the houses that you have labour in the country to build?' On the face of it, that seems as if it were an unbusinesslike thing to do, but there are two very substantial reasons why we should do it. The first is, that the houses to be built under the present arrangements are, first of all, for people who can afford to purchase houses or people who can afford to pay a fairly high rent for the houses. In other words, there are houses being produced for the people who require them least. It is the people who require them least who are getting these houses either by purchase or by paying high rents. I submit that if there were no poorer people in the country than the people who are now getting houses there would be no housing problem, and there certainly would be no State subsidies for house building. It is because we have a great multitude, a necessary, important, valuable multitude, who are poorer than these, who cannot afford either to buy or to rent healthy houses at an economic rent, that we have a housing problem at all. As things stand today it is the people who do not need our help for whom houses are provided. In order to provide for the people who do need our help, in order to

Is it reasonable to expect these people to be enthusiastic about building houses which are closed to them, into which they and their class may never hope to enter.

widen the range, to enlarge the areas from where tenants may be drawn, we require to extend our subsidy, to bring rents down to a level which these people can afford to pay. That is the first substantial reason.

The second is that, unless you bring in this great multitude who require houses at low rents, you cannot give to the building industry that guarantee of continued employment which is necessary, and these certainly are two very substantial reasons which justify the giving of a higher subsidy. There is another point. Included in the class for whom you cannot get houses today are the very people who build houses. The bricklayer and the bricklayers' labourers cannot afford to purchase houses which the bricklayer and the bricklayers' labourers are building, nor can they afford to pay the high rents which are now being charged for these houses, that is for the very small number of them that are being let. That is well known to hon Members in all parts of the House. Is it reasonable to expect these people to be enthusiastic about building houses which are closed to them, into which they and their class may never hope to enter. Is it reasonable to expect them to have that enthusiasm which you want to engender in them for the building of these houses?

If the building workers are to refrain from exacting their pound of flesh to the uttermost, that economic pound which the shortage of labour enables them to demand, are they not reasonably entitled to ask you to refrain from charging the last penny for the rent of the houses, especially when charging the last penny puts a fence between them and the house? Again, if you are going to lay down that, because you could possibly get a pound more for a house, you are entitled to take it, what case have you against the brick manufacturer who says that he can get a pound more for his bricks when you ask him to take less? What have you to do to solve the housing problem? You have to produce houses, and healthy houses, at rents which the multitude of this country can afford to pay for houses...

> Is it reasonable to expect these people to be enthusiastic about building houses which are closed to them, into which they and their class may never hope to enter.

The hon and gallant Member [Walter Elliot] now represents a Division of the City of Glasgow [Kelvingrove]. I know something of that Division, and he will agree with me that it contains some of worst slums in the city, perhaps some of the worst slums in the world. Would the hon and gallant Member suggest that the local authorities of Lanarkshire and Glasgow are reactionary local authorities? Are they not among the most progressive local authorities in the country? They have not been building under the 1923 Act, because they found that they could not do so. What has happened since? Since this House passed the Money Resolution for this Bill the Housing Committee of the Glasgow Corporation have unanimously recommended their Finance Committee to raise a loan of £3,000,000 to enable them to proceed with the erection of 6,000 or 7,000 of the houses formulated in that proposal. That is the new spirit which is coming in, and, in conclusion, I would say that that spirit and this Bill will solve the housing problem.

Look neither to the right nor to the left, but keep straight on.

HH Asquith
1852–1928

SPEECH TO LIBERAL ACTIVISTS • GREENOCK
15 OCTOBER 1926

By the autumn of 1926 Herbert Henry Asquith was in failing health. In June that year he had suffered a mild stroke that incapacitated him for three months, a malaise mirrored within the Liberal Party, still riven by a long-running feud with another former Prime Minister and party leader, David Lloyd George. The latter period of Asquith's leadership, wrote his biographer Roy Jenkins, 'had been a painful and protracted business. He had stayed too long in an impossible situation.'[14]

Herbert Henry Asquith, 1st Earl of Oxford and Asquith, was born in 1852 and served as Prime Minister from 1908–16. Initially, he led his Liberal Party in a series of domestic reforms, including social security and taming the House of Lords, but he is chiefly remembered as a rather ineffectual leader during the First World War. Asquith also served as Home Secretary and Chancellor. He died in 1928, having represented two Scottish constituencies, East Fife and Paisley.

Publicly, Asquith announced his resignation in a short letter to the heads of the English and Scottish Liberal Federations. This was published on 15 October, and that same night he had arranged a farewell meeting at Greenock. He travelled to Scotland with a large party including leading Liberals, who joined members of his family on the platform.

'The meeting in Greenock,' wrote Asquith a couple of days later, 'was unique in my experience: at moments thrilling in its intensity. There were a lot of my old and trusty friends from Paisley there, as well as good and true men and women from all parts of Scotland. It was sad, however necessary, to have to cause so much pain. But I have not a doubt that I have taken the only wise and honourable course.' Just 16 months later, Asquith was dead.

I DID NOT FORESEE, nor did any of you, that the date selected so long ago for this gathering would be the morrow of my own resignation of the leadership of the Liberal Party. You will believe me when I say it is not a light thing, to be done precipitately, without the fullest reflection, and even then with the utmost reluctance, to abandon a post of such honour as the leadership of a great historic party. I have set out in the letter which most, and probably all, of you will have read this morning the reasons which led me, after most patient and careful deliberation, to take so serious a step...

Let me say also, if the time for laying down the leadership had to come, there could be no more appropriate place than at a meeting of Liberal delegates from all parts of Scotland. The whole of my House of Commons career was passed as a Scottish member. I never stood or sat for any constituency in my native country, but I was for over 30 years the representative of an Eastern county, or rather kingdom, for such we call it in Fife. When the men of the last thought fit to sever our long connection, I turned to the West and found a welcome refuge among your neighbours at Paisley. I represented Paisley for the best part of five years, during which I had what is, I suppose, a unique experience, for I fought no fewer than four contested elections. It is a melancholy fact, melancholy to me at least, that the Scottish electorate, East and West, has twice shown that it had had

> Scotland has unlocked for me the avenue to the leadership, and it is only fitting it should be in Scotland that I bid the leadership farewell.

enough of me; but I cherish no resentment. I feel nothing, as I look back on all those years of close and intimate association with the fighting Liberals of Scotland, but admiration and gratitude for their devoted loyalty, their sturdy and robust political sense, and, I will add, for the informed and reasoned political faith which has always given to Scottish Liberalism a brand and character of its own. Scotland unlocked for me the avenue to the leadership, and it is only fitting it should be in Scotland that I bid the leadership farewell...

Men come and go – As one of our poets has said: –

> Wave following wave departs for ever,
> But still flows the eternal river.[15]

Men come and go. The fortunes of parties...fluctuate and oscillate in what often seems a most capricious and haphazard fashion. The Liberal Party has this advantage, an advantage which I claim for it as against all competitive parties in the State, that it can point to the richest record of actual achievement in the removal of abuses and the extension of freedom, in securing, step by step, that predominance of the general over the particular interest, which I have described as one of its great principles. You have only to look at the Statute-book to find

> Keep that faith, carry on the torch which we, who have done our best to keep it alight, hand over to your custody.

there written in indelible letters what Liberalism, supported by the opinion of the country, really means, and what it can do in increasing the happiness and enlarging the freedom of the great masses of our citizens...

Let none of you, and especially let none of the younger among you, be content to think that the mission of Liberalism is exhausted. The new problems which confront us, and they are many and grave, are not outside the ambit of the old faith. Keep that faith, carry on the torch which we, who have done our best to keep it alight, hand over to your custody. Resist all the allurements of short cuts and compromises. Look neither to the right nor to the left, but keep straight on.

There is nothing better for an old Scottish song than that it should be sung over again.

Rev James Barr
1862–1949

SPEECH MOVING SECOND READING OF THE
GOVERNMENT OF SCOTLAND BILL • HOUSE OF COMMONS

13 MAY 1927

Initially a Liberal, James Barr entered Parliament as the Labour MP for Motherwell in 1924, just after the first – albeit brief – Labour government had left office. Although he was not unique among Presbyterian ministers in having embraced socialism, Barr was certainly in a minority, as most of his contemporaries were strongly antagonistic to the Labour Party.

In supporting devolution for Scotland, however, Barr was on safer political terrain. A founder and past president of the Scottish Home Rule Association, this speech comes from the Second Reading debate on his own Government of Scotland Bill, introduced to Parliament in 1927. It was not the first, but it came at a time when – and indeed perhaps helped stimulate – Nationalist sentiment was growing in Scotland. The Secretary for Scotland, meanwhile, had recently been elevated to a full Secretary of State by the Prime Minister, Stanley Baldwin.

Rev James Barr was born in 1862 in Ayrshire. He was educated at Kilmarnock Academy and Glasgow University. After a year touring North America recovering from a breakdown, Barr took up a scholarship at Trinity College, Glasgow, the college of the United Free Church, to study for the ministry. Initially a Liberal, Barr was elected the Labour MP for Motherwell in 1924. He died in 1949.

Barr looked like a farmer; a tall, powerful man, and an equally powerful speaker. He proposed a single Scottish legislature composed of 148 members, two elected from each extant Westminster constituency. The arguments deployed for devolution were familiar, even in 1927, and would be rehearsed again and again until the matter was settled – at least momentarily – in 1999.

THE BILL PROCEEDS on the principle of self-determination. It proceeds throughout on the basis of Scotland being a sovereign state. We may well wonder that separate legislatures for different parts of this country have not been set up sooner... It was as far back as 1889 that Dr Clark brought forward a Measure of Scottish Home Rule. It was in an uncongenial atmosphere but,

notwithstanding that, on the very first trial, so far as Scottish representation was
concerned, he almost carried a majority, the Scottish Members voting being 22
against and 19 for...

> *It is because we believe today that none*
> *can save Scotland but Scotland's self that we ask*
> *for a Second Reading of this Measure.*

What I have been showing is that, whether this House voted for or against
Home Rule, ever since the first trial in 1899 we have had a large preponderance of
Scottish representatives who took part in the vote going in favour of Home Rule.
I find that the *Glasgow Herald* and other Scottish papers are indicating that the
problem is already sufficiently met by the new status which has been given to the
Secretary for Scotland. I think that really shows rather a low estimation of the
vastness of the problem we have to deal with and a rather high estimation of the
miracle that has been wrought by giving a new title to the Secretary for Scotland...

The question of housing presents a most grave problem in Scotland. We are
waiting for the organisation, the supervision and the uplift which only a national
Parliament could give. I have referred to the Church. If it had gone by the vote of
the Scottish representatives in 1843 there would have been no disruption in the
Church at all and the course of Church history would have been different; for 25
Scottish Members voted for Fox Maule's Motion and 12 against. With regard to
education, we do not do any boasting... In regard to recent Acts, particularly of
superannuation, we have been warned, even by Labour Secretaries for Scotland
and on all sides, that we must keep strictly in step with England. Owing to the
custom by which we get 11/80ths of what is spent we have a Board of Education
in Scotland which is parsimonious in the same sense and degree as that in
England...

> *Our whole literature pulsates with the*
> *passion for Scottish freedom and Scottish nationality.*

I would like to say two other things. Our whole literature pulsates with the
passion for Scottish freedom and Scottish nationality... The last point is that we
are seeking to restore, in a more effective form I trust, the right that we have to
the independent Parliament that was ours. That Parliament has an ancient and
honourable history. It goes back to the year 1326. Its influence was impaired by
the Union of the Crowns. James VI, writing from England, said: 'Here I sit and
govern Scotland with my pen. I write and it is done; and by the Clerk of the
Council I govern Scotland now, which others could not do by the sword.' These
words would be very appropriate to the Secretary of State for Scotland, who is the

James VI of our time. When that Parliament was taken from us, it was against the protests of the whole nation. The Royal Burghs were against it. The General Assembly of the Church appointed a special National Fast. The Cameronians, the most stalwart of the Covenanters, to the number of 200 met in the streets of Dumfries and burned the Articles of Union at the Market Cross. In Glasgow, which has not altogether lost its sturdy character, there were riots, and Daniel Defoe said that Scotland had gone mad against the Measure. Plato says that there is a certain divine madness and I believe that it was such madness which existed then. We lost the Parliament by wholesale bribery...

On the occasion of almost the last meeting of the Scottish Parliament, on the 2 November 1706, when the Parliament was as good as lost, Lord Belhaven said: 'None can destroy Scotland, save Scotland's self.' It is because we believe today that none can save Scotland but Scotland's self that we ask for a Second Reading of this Measure. Another famous saying was spoken by Lord Chancellor Seafield, on the 25 March 1707, at the last meeting of the old Scottish Parliament, when he said: 'There is the end of an auld sang.' Hon Members will grant that there is nothing better for an old Scottish song than that it should be sung over again. We propose that it should be sung over again in richer, fuller and clearer notes, to call the people of Scotland to new hope and a higher and nobler endeavour.

*It connotes a journey,
this one not from Lambeth to Bedford,
but from St Paul's to St Peter's.*

Edward Rosslyn Mitchell
1879–1965

SPEECH ON PRAYER BOOK MEASURE • HOUSE OF COMMONS

13 JUNE 1928

Edward Rosslyn Mitchell is now almost forgotten, but in 1924 he caused a political sensation by defeating the Liberal leader and former Prime Minister HH Asquith in Paisley by 2,228 votes. Unfortunately, once in Parliament, Mitchell proved something of a disappointment, making only a few notable interventions in debates, mainly on Scottish housing.

The exception was this 1928 speech, which opposed the revision of the *Book of Common Prayer*. Mitchell had already lambasted the proposed changes in Parliament the previous year, arguing that it was 'papistical' and amounted to a restoration of the Roman Mass. Early in 1928 the book, with some amendments, was again passed by a large majority in the Church of England Assembly, but the resolution directing that it be presented to His Majesty then had to be debated in the Commons.

Edward Rosslyn Mitchell was born in Devizes, Wiltshire, the son of a celebrated evangelical preacher. He studied law at the University of Glasgow and thereafter practiced as a solicitor. Initially a Liberal, he contested Buteshire in 1910, but joined the ILP in 1918 and was elected the Labour MP for Paisley in 1924. Mitchell quit the Commons in 1929, returned to local Glasgow politics and died in 1965.

Regarded by some as one of the most outstanding examples of oratory heard in the House of Commons in the 20th century, Mitchell's contribution certainly fizzles with righteous indignation. It proved effective; the motion was defeated, and in response the bishops issued a statement asserting the Church's right to order its form of worship.

THE CHURCH OF ENGLAND is different from any other Church. The Church of England is really a sort of representative Church of the whole people of England. It is not a case simply of cities in which you can go from one street to another if you do not like the church you are attending. In so many of the small towns and villages of England there is only one church and there is only one school, and if it be the case that the vicar of that church, who is a very important person in the school, takes the Anglo-Catholic view of this Book and teaches the children in that village certain doctrines and inculcates in their minds certain practices which are entirely antagonistic to the point of view of their parents, those children must either continue to go to receive that instruction which their parents detest, or they must be excluded altogether. It is a very important thing. The only reason why the establishment of the Church of England is acquiesced in by the people of England is that in doctrine and outlook the Church of England has remained fundamentally Protestant...

The whole tendency is towards Rome. The emphasis is towards Rome. I know it is not all the way. It is only a milestone, but a milestone connotes a journey from somewhere to somewhere. It connotes a journey, this one not from Lambeth to Bedford, but from St Paul's to St Peter's. There are other milestones. One was covered up, the Malines milestone, in which the Papacy was recognised, in which Transubstantiation was declared; and the other milestone has been given us tonight and is in all our minds – the declaration of 2,229 of the priests

> I am, personally, the most Catholic soul alive, but I am not Roman Catholic.

of the Church of England that, no matter what we do here, they are going to hold and, if they hold, promote the doctrine of the complete Transubstantiation.

I cannot possibly regard this as anything but a definite trend of emphasis for a change in the doctrine and practice of the Church of England as a Protestant Church to the Church of England as a Catholic Church, and a Roman Catholic Church. Tomorrow the House has to make a very definite and deliberate decision, and tomorrow is a day not without significance in the history of this country. Two hundred and eighty-three years ago tomorrow there was fought the Battle of Naseby,[16] and I pray God that the deliberations and decision of this House tomorrow may be guided as I believe the decision of that conflict was guided then.

I am, personally, the most Catholic soul alive, but I am not Roman Catholic, and I do not want the Church of England to become Roman Catholic. If it does, its existence as an Established Church becomes impossible. If we do not pass this Book, there may be a secession; if we do pass this Book, there may be a disruption, and the Church of England may be left no longer as a national Church, but simply as a sect, and it cannot continue to exist as an Established Church if it remains a priestly sect instead of the expression of the religious views and instincts of the people. Therefore, if the Book is passed and that disruption takes place, the good people of England will sweep away the Establishment, and the Church of England will be worse off than ever it has been before.

Nationality is in the atmosphere of the world.

RB Cunninghame Graham
1852–1936

SPEECH AT BANNOCKBURN DEMONSTRATION • STIRLING

21 JUNE 1930

The flamboyant RB Cunninghame Graham was one of the earliest espousers of the Scottish Nationalist cause. He had promoted Home Rule for Scotland (and Ireland) since entering Parliament as the Liberal MP for North-West Lanarkshire in 1886. When asked in the House of Commons whether he preached 'pure unmitigated Socialism', he replied: 'Undoubtedly.'

Robert Bontine Cunninghame Graham was born into an army family in 1852. He was educated at Harrow but, aged 17, set out for South America where he worked in cattle ranching and horse dealing. In 1886 he became the Liberal MP for North-West Lanarkshire, although arguably he was Parliament's first socialist Member. Cunninghame Graham wrote and travelled widely, and died in 1936.

Later, Cunninghame Graham dabbled in Labour politics, but his views changed again during the First World War and he stood unsuccessfully as a Liberal at Western Stirling and Clackmannan in 1918. Thereafter he devoted his political energies to the cause of Scottish home rule, becoming president of the Scottish Home Rule Association and of its successor, the National Party of Scotland. When, in 1934, the National Party was merged with the Duke of Montrose's more right-wing Scottish Party to become the Scottish National Party, Cunninghame Graham remained president until his death.

Prior to 1934, and indeed to this day, Scottish Nationalists held their annual demonstration at Stirling. At that held in 1930, from which this speech is taken, a large crowd marched from the Station Road to the King's Park, where they signed a covenant pledging to do everything possible to secure Scottish sovereignty. Cunninghame Graham's speech was, according to a *Scotsman* reporter, 'vigorous'. Below is the speech as reported by the newspaper.

[HE] SAID THAT THE scenes around him stirred the heart, and made one feel that they were representatives of a distinct nationality – a nationality separate from all nationalities and as different to their friends in England as they were from the Germans, the French, the Russians, or any other nationality in Europe. (Applause.) The British Empire today had become a confederation of varying states. Australia, New Zealand, British Colombia, the Cape Colonies, and all the rest of the Dependencies had got their Parliaments and separate legislators. They were all practically self-governing States within their boundaries, and he asked: – Was Scotland inferior to any one of those States? Did they not send out the best and bravest of their sons to colonise Canada, New Zealand, Australia, and wherever the flag of the British Empire floated? He asked them as Scotsmen and Scottish women whether it was not an injustice that cried to heaven – a sin against political science – that the one nationality, perhaps the oldest of all those he had enumerated, older perhaps than even England itself as a separate State, should be subservient, should be a mere appendage of the predominant partner, a mere county of England.

Nationality, he declared, was in the atmosphere of the world. Within the last ten years they had seen 20 nationalities come into being. Was Scotland to lag behind? They talked about the prayer for a good conceit of themselves, and he used to think it was a prayer that was scarcely worth putting up by Scotsmen, but today it was a prayer that every Scotsman and Scottish woman should keep in mind and should perpetually put up until they had achieved that which they had in view – complete autonomy for their native land. (Applause.) He laid upon

> All that was left for them was to bow to the golden calf of England and to kiss the rod that chastised them.

them as a sacred duty to agitate and agitate until their old Parliament was restored to them and once again Scotland took her place as an independent nationality in the family of nations. (Applause.) No responsible statesman, no highly placed member of any of the parties, had devoted a speech or a motion in the House of Commons or introduced legislation touching exclusively with Scotland, and therefore he concluded that it was a sham for Scotsmen to look for help in their struggle for autonomy to any of the existing parties. (Applause.)

The prosperity of Scotland was induced by the economic progress of the world. It was not in England's power, even if she had wished to do so, to withhold the benefits which naturally accrued by the increasing wealth of Europe from Scotland. Scotland merely followed in the same development that touched France, Germany, Italy, even Spain, and certainly the United States. Those who wished to take them back to the old times and paint a derogatory portrait of Scotland were not true Scotsmen, were not true lovers of their own country, and all that was left for them was to bow to the golden calf of England and to kiss the rod that chastised them. (Applause.) Concluding, Mr Cunninghame Graham said there were many ways in which they could achieve self-government and autonomy for Scotland. They were not asked to endure death, imprisonment, as were the Irish. It was merely a simple process. They had merely got to vote and Scottish Home Rule would be as certain as day followed night.

When I see this sort of thing I say, God help me, I am for none of it!

Edwin Scrymgeour
1866–1947

SPEECH DURING DEBATE ON 'ANOMALIES' BILL • HOUSE OF COMMONS

21 JULY 1931

E dwin Scrymgeour was primarily a prohibitionist, and he sensationally defeated Winston Churchill in Dundee at the 1922 general election on that platform. In the House of Commons, he aligned himself with the ILP, but the period of the second Labour government (1929–31) convinced Scrymgeour that its leadership was moving away from socialism and was, in his eyes, becoming insensitive to the sufferings of the unemployed.

Edwin Scrymgeour was born in Dundee, the fifth of eight children of James Scrymgeour, a temperance and charity worker. For some years he combined work and prohibitionist politics, and in 1901 became a founder member of the Scottish Prohibition Party. Scrymgeour was elected to Dundee town council in 1905 and contested Dundee several times before entering Parliament in 1922. He lost his seat in 1931 and worked for the rest of his life as a hospital chaplain.

In 1930 he remarked witheringly that the 'game of party politics is being played by the Labour Party just as readily as by any other party'.[17] The Minister of Labour's 'Anomalies' Bill, which sought to reduce the cost of unemployment benefit during a period of rising joblessness, was the final straw. Rising to address the Chamber, Scrymgeour condemned the Bill, and also the Labour government for attacking (as he saw it) the weakest and poorest section of society.

S OME PEOPLE ARE getting unemployment benefit who ought not to get it. We do not know who they are, but there are suspicions, and all the three parties are reckoned to have become consolidated on this, that, to use the right hon Lady's [Margaret Bondfield's] phrase, they are going on an exploration expedition to discover those who may have been getting benefit who ought not to have got it. The travesty of the whole situation, particularly for a Labour Government, is to me appalling. I can quite understand the difficulty as to the Baronets, but that does not get over the central point of the whole thing, which concerns the men and women who are unemployed and who are likely not to get benefit...

It is a chase after a mouse. The Government seemingly are pledged to grapple with the great anomalies, but the one amazing anomaly, in the midst of the scientific advancement in this and other civilised countries, which we have not settled is the question of enabling people to live. It is an amazing spectacle.

And yet we have reports specifically bearing upon the underlying question of how people are doing under our financial system. We have the Prime Minister and the Chancellor of the Exchequer saying that we are not going to have any discussion, not even any talk, about a matter which it is said is of the utmost importance and yet must be postponed. We are not to have any elucidation after all the investigation by experts of the underlying factor, the financial issue...

I do not want to give a silent vote. I am not making any attempt to indulge in what may be called fireworks or anything of that sort from a Parliamentary point of view. I can see that steady queue of suffering men and women gradually dropping away from the Exchanges unable to get benefit, living in appalling conditions, and we are utterly unable to tell them where they can get work or to do anything for them at all. They are looking to the Government to deal resolutely with the issues.

> In the midst of the scientific advancement
> in this and other civilised countries, which we have not
> settled is the question of enabling people to live.

The constituency which I represent is going deeper and deeper into misery. Big concerns are losing their business, masses of people are unable to get the chance of a look-in, and the Government's explanation is that, even at the best, they do not expect that very much can come out of it all. To me it is an ignominious failure on the part of the Labour forces. They are going deeper and deeper into the way of saying: 'We have to follow the lines of orthodox political propaganda. The House is faced with powerful forces with which it cannot cope. We have to try to work on the old fashioned lines.' The once Liberal or Radical party becomes now the Labour party, and it becomes consolidated while the squeeze still proceeds on the lines of this Bill. (Interruption.) When you come here you have to forget those you represent. I know that kind of Parliamentary movement. I find men getting appointments here, and then snapping their fingers at the struggles outside. I know what is going on, perfectly well. I know about the buttressing of the whole political situation. The Labour party as a great moral propaganda, as a great moral movement, is failing because so many members of it find it so convenient to follow along the tracks that other men have followed. The motto is: 'Take things easy. Do not fight, do not struggle for those outside.' So far as I am concerned, when I see this sort of thing I say, God help me, I am for none of it!

I believe that Scotland is about to live with a fullness of life undreamed of yet.

Sir Compton Mackenzie
1883–1972

RECTORIAL ADDRESS · UNIVERSITY OF GLASGOW

29 JANUARY 1932

The writer Compton Mackenzie – most famous for his comic novel *Whisky Galore* (1947) – was a founder member of the National Party of Scotland in 1928 and his election in 1931 as the first ever Nationalist Rector of a Scottish university was seen as a major boost to a then fledgling political party. 'I am the first Catholic Rector to be elected since the Reformation,' Mackenzie wrote to his mother, 'and the first literary man since Macaulay, but he was a politician as well.'

Sir (Edward Montague Anthony) Compton Mackenzie was born in West Hartlepool in 1883 to a theatrical family. He was educated at St Paul's School and Magdalen College, Oxford, and he concentrated on writing after abandoning his training for the English Bar. Several novels and memoirs followed, but from the 1920s Mackenzie looked increasingly towards Scotland. He died in Edinburgh in 1972.

Mackenzie agreed to give his Rectorial address on 29 January 1932, the centenary of Goethe's death. The week before he fell ill with severe flu, but after taking several pills, including strychnine, he managed to deliver it. Mackenzie's sister Fay, appearing in pantomime in Glasgow, described the scene for his mother: 'It is a most remarkable tribute to him that during the long reading of his address, the students were practically silent – there were just a few harmless interruptions.'

Andro Linklater reckoned Mackenzie's speech 'was the distillation of everything he held most important, and he had agonised over its construction as though it were a novel'. Mackenzie explained that Scottish Nationalism was the natural outcome of a war that had been fought over the rights of small nations. When he had finished, his sister recalled 'such cheering and enthusiasm' that she 'felt tremendously proud and again very close to tears'.[18]

NATIONALISM IN ITS political aspect is essentially a reactionary theory of government. It is the admission by the part of an inability to adjust itself to the whole. It is reactionary too in its opposition to centralisation, the upholders of which can claim that man's ascent in evolution is the result of centralising its nervous system. Reaction, however, should be only temporary, hardly more than the ebb of the tide before it flows again. Nationalism desires to perfect the parts before it allows progress to move forward to achieve the perfect whole. The present threat to ultimate perfection is the too ready sacrifice of backward or imperfect parts to achieve a premature centralisation which when achieved will diffuse not life but death. Nationalism is a demand by the soul of man to afford him leisure for the contemplation of his own destiny, to restore to him a richer personal life, and by narrowing his background to enable him to recover a measure of his own significance in time and space...

If nationalism be something more than a sentimental emotion it must be able to fight for itself in the arena of mundane tendencies. I have too infrangible a faith in the spiritual destiny of man to propose that Scotland should retire from the struggle in order to preserve an ignominious unimportance as a small nation on the edge of the great Eurasian continent. If I suggest that she should step back, it is because I believe that by stepping back and living upon herself she can

... because I believe that Scotland is about to live with a fullness of life undreamed of yet, that I count it the proudest moment of my career to be standing here today.

leap forward to the spiritual and intellectual leadership of mankind. It is not because I believe that Scotland is dying, but because I believe that Scotland is about to live with a fullness of life undreamed of yet, that I count it the proudest moment of my career to be standing here today...

While night after night I have been struggling to put into words these reflections, of the inadequacy of which to such an occasion I am bitterly conscious, there has lain upon my table a volume whose pages are spongy and thumbed with the hard reading of careless boyhood. That volume is Scott's *Tales of a Grandfather*, presented to me in January on my seventh birthday. To the hours of youth spent in reading and re-reading those pages I owe the honour of standing here almost exactly 42 years later, for I was born again in that book, never a page of which reminded me that 150 sundering years lay between myself and my natural background.

... in that sight of Glasgow something added which neither Rome nor Athens could give – the glory and grandeur of the future.

It happened that soon after I became possessed of this talisman to live in the past of that race from which I was sprung I travelled northward alone. It was near dusk on the evening of earliest spring. Somebody in the railway-carriage announced that we were crossing the border, and I craned my head out of the window to enjoy the magical sensation. Down the long train came a faint sound of cheering, and from windows far ahead I could see hats being waved. An austere landscape in the fast-fading dusk, a steam of flamy smoke from an engine, a few cheers ringing thinly above the roar of a train, a waving of hats: not much perhaps, but enough for a child of eight to sit back again in a dim railway-carriage and dream over, his heart blazoned like a herald's tabard with the bright symbols of his country's life, his heart draped like a hatchment with the sombre memories of defeat upon defeat. Thence onward I lived secretly in the past of my country; but because through the closing years of the 19th century and through the opening years of the 20th the future of which I was dreaming seemed as improbable as a Jacobite hope, as fruitless as a white rose reverie, I did what so many sons of Scotland were doing and abandoned myself to the pursuit of material success in that larger world which seemed to be submerging the smaller

> If nationalism be something more than a sentimental emotion it must be able to fight for itself in the arena of mundane tendencies.

nations. Yet, some intuition of the future must have prevented my squandering any of those more intimate aspirations on the merely literary expression of them. I shall not weary you with a map of the devious paths by which through a quarter of a century of what I think I may without presumption call an existence of unusual variety and fullness I reached the point at which by other paths enough of my countrymen had already arrived to give me the assurance that I was not an isolated eccentric. The vision of Scotland which as a boy I had beheld in the *Tales of a Grandfather* was no longer a dream that faded when the book was closed; it was omnipresent in the daily round of life...

I have seen the phenomenon of conversion among those who have wakened to a sudden comprehension of what true nationalism is. They are changed by some mystical experience, and in loving their country they love their fellow-countrymen. It is such a love which alone can justify the reformer. Too many attempts at reformation have been made either in a spirit of hate and destructiveness or, what is ultimately more deadly, in a spirit of constructive

> Nationalism desires to perfect the parts before it allows progress to move forward to achieve the perfect whole.

utility. Desire the good of your fellow men, but desire it because you love them, not because a well-fed, well-clad, well-housed creature will be an economic asset to the state. Many of you present are filled with ambition to re-create a nation; but your immediate and predominant duty is to re-create yourselves, for only in re-creating yourselves will you re-create that nation...

A few weeks ago upon the Campsie Fells I gazed down at Glasgow. From a mass of dark cloud the sun, himself obscured from where I stood, sloped his golden ladders into that rain-washed city, which lay with all her spires and chimneys, with all her towers and tenements and sparkling roofs, like a vision of heavenly habitations. I have looked down over Athens. I have looked down over Rome. With beauty unparagoned the glory and the grandeur of the past have been spread before my eyes; but in that sight of Glasgow something was added which neither Rome nor Athens could give – the glory and the grandeur of the future, and the beating heart of a nation.

I believe that every Scotsman should be a Scottish Nationalist.

John Buchan
1875–1940

SPEECH DURING DEBATE ON THE ADDRESS • HOUSE OF COMMONS

24 NOVEMBER 1932

Publishing is my business,' John Buchan often remarked, 'writing my amusement and politics my duty.' Nevertheless, it is often forgotten that the author of *The Thirty-Nine Steps* was also a Scottish Conservative MP, representing one of the three Combined Scottish Universities seats from 1927 until standing down on his appointment as governor-general of Canada in 1935.

In truth, Buchan was frustrated at persistently being overlooked for office, perhaps because he was perceived to be too busy writing novels. He spoke sparingly in Parliament, but when he did intervene he did so with authority. Although Scottish Nationalists have claimed Buchan as one of their own, he was in fact what his biographer Andrew Lownie calls 'an enlightened Unionist, prepared to cloak his own views in rhetoric'[19] to give it broader appeal.

John Buchan, 1st Baron Tweedsmuir, was a Scottish novelist, historian and Unionist politician. After a brief career as a lawyer, he mixed writing with his political and diplomatic career, serving as private secretary to various colonial administrators in Southern Africa. Buchan was appointed governor-general of Canada in 1935 and occupied that post until his death in 1940, upon which he received a state funeral.

This speech is a case in point. By 1932 there were discernable signs of a growing Nationalist movement in Scotland, and Buchan responded by analysing why Scots felt disenfranchised and attempted to put forward a solution. This was a 'sane nationalism', urging more administrative devolution to a Scottish Office based in Edinburgh (this came to pass in 1939) and a specifically 'Scottish' government policy.

MANY ARGUMENTS BROUGHT against Scottish Home Rule are merely foolish. We are told sometimes that a Scottish Parliament would be a fiasco and that it would be a kind of enlarged, noisy, incompetent town council. What earthly warrant is there for that view? The Scottish people, with a long tradition of democracy in their bones, are at least as capable of running a parliament successfully as any other race. Moreover, we all know that there is in Scotland today a great deal of public spirit and administrative ability which, for various reasons, cannot find an outlet in this Parliament, but might, in a domestic legislature.

Let us get rid also, once for all, of the absurd argument that because Scotsmen are successful in England and in the Empire and take a large part in their maintenance, it does not matter what happens to Scotland. It is not with what Scotsmen outside are doing that we are concerned, but with Scotland herself. That argument misses the whole point. Many people believe, rightly or wrongly, that there is a danger of Scotland sinking to the position of a mere Northern province of England...

I believe that every Scotsman should be a Scottish Nationalist. If it could be proved that a separate Scottish Parliament were desirable, that is to say that the merits were greater than the disadvantages and dangers, Scotsmen should support it. I would go further. Even if it were not proved desirable, if it could be proved to be desired by any substantial majority of the Scottish people, then Scotland should be allowed to make the experiment, and I do not believe that, England would desire for one moment to stand in the way...

The main force clearly in the [Nationalist] movement is what might be called the cultural force, the desire that Scotland shall not lose her historic personality.

If we attempt to localize them, we shall lay the axe to the root of all healthy development.

I am afraid that people in cultural movements are always apt to run to machinery for a solution. Machinery will never effect a cultural revival. I would remind the House that the greatest moment in Scottish literary and artistic history was at the end of the 18th century when Scotland was under the iron heel of Henry Dundas.[20] To imagine that a cultural revival will gush from the establishment of a separate legislature is like digging a well without making an inquiry into the presence of water-bearing strata...

The conclusion to which I have been forced is that, real as the needs are, to attempt to meet them by creating an elaborate independent legislature would be more than those needs require. Such a top-heavy structure would not cure Scotland's ills; it would intensify them. It would create artificial differences, hinder co-operation, and engender friction if we attempted to split up services which Scotland has had in common with England for 200 years. Today the industrial problems of all Britain are closely related, and, if we attempt to localise them, we shall lay the axe to the root of all healthy development. It is our business to realise that, while Scotland is a nation in a true sense, she is also a nation in the closest corporate alliance with her Southern neighbour in most practical matters, and to attempt to separate them would be a costly blunder. I do not believe, and no Scotsman believes, in spending money without a proper return. Further, I believe that it would produce a far more sinister result – it would check the hope of that true material and spiritual development which Scotland needs, by turning her attention from the things which really matter to the barren task of working a clumsy and unnecessary machine...

But the problem is insistent, and must be faced... In the future it may be necessary to go further; I do not know; I have no gift of prophecy. But if we assert our national individuality, and give it a visible form in our administration, at any rate we are creating a foundation on which can be built any structure which the needs of the future may require.

We do not want to be like the Jews of Dispersion, a potent force everywhere on the globe, but with no Jerusalem.

May I be allowed to say one word to my friends who regard this whole question as trivial – trivial compared with the great economic problems with which we are faced today? I do not deny for a moment the gravity of these other problems, but, believe me, this question is not trivial; it goes to the very root of the future not only of Scotland but of Britain and of the Empire. Britain cannot afford, the Empire cannot afford, I do not think the world can afford, a denationalised Scotland. In Sir Walter Scott's famous words, 'If you un-Scotch us, you will make us damned mischievous Englishmen.'[21] We do not want to be, like the Greeks, powerful and prosperous wherever we settle, but with a dead Greece behind us. We do not want to be like the Jews of the Dispersion – a potent force everywhere on the globe, but with no Jerusalem.

It has never been done better by a woman before, and, whatever else may be said about me, in the future from henceforward I am historic.

Florence Horsbrugh
1889–1969

SPEECH MOVING THE DEBATE ON THE ADDRESS • HOUSE OF COMMONS

3 NOVEMBER 1936

Florence Horsbrugh was already well known for her wartime work in 'national kitchens' by the time she entered Parliament in 1931. She had won the nomination for the apparently hopeless two-member seat of Dundee, but her sense of humour and talent as a public speaker got her through a gruelling campaign. The unusual circumstances of that general election, which returned the National Government to power with a landslide majority, meant Horsbrugh was able to overturn a Labour majority of 14,000.

As an MP, she made an immediate impression on the House with her maiden speech, apparently delivered impromptu, on the Abnormal Importations Bill, during which she placed great emphasis on solving unemployment by using tariffs to exclude imported goods. Foreshadowing Margaret Thatcher, Horsbrugh emphasised her status as an MP rather than a women's representative, arguing that it would not help the cause for Members to be relegated to women's questions.

In 1936, after Dundee had returned her for a second time, Horsbrugh became the first female Member of Parliament to move the Address in reply to the King's Speech. As a public speaker, she enjoyed 'the advantage of a resonant, well-modulated voice and a tall, dignified bearing' and, on this occasion, wore evening dress as she spoke.

Florence Gertrude Horsbrugh was born in Edinburgh and educated there and at St Hilda's in Folkestone. After several years in Parliament she finally became a junior minister at the Ministry of Health on the eve of the Second World War. She lost her Dundee seat in 1945 but was returned for Manchester Moss Side in 1951, and became Minister for Education in Churchill's last government.

THE FACT THAT THE Member selected for this honourable and onerous duty is a woman has, I believe, been appreciated as a compliment not only to the women Members of this House but to the vast number of women electors throughout the country. I will not liken this occasion to the crumbling of some fortress wall which has defended the citadel of male prerogative, for, being a native of Edinburgh, I must beware of using a military metaphor lest I bring to the minds of hon Members an epithet, somewhat ungallant, used by that stern Scottish reformer, John Knox, when describing organised womanhood in his day.[22] I prefer to think of this occasion as the opening of a gate into a new field of opportunity, and I believe the gate is being thrown open with true, if somewhat

In war time there comes a distinct cleavage between the burdens of suffering each is called upon to bear.

tardy, hospitality. If in these new and novel surroundings I acquit myself but poorly, when I sit down I shall at least have two thoughts for my consolation – it has never been done better by a woman before, and, whatever else may be said about me, in the future from henceforward I am historic.

The legislative programme outlined in the Gracious Speech will be welcomed by the people of this country with a sense of satisfaction and relief. The programme is designed to bring greater security to individual citizens, to the economic and political life of the country and to the nation as a whole. We are all rejoiced to read: 'the general trade and industrial outlook continues to be favourable, and that there is good ground for expecting that there will be further improvement.' As the Special Areas Act is to be extended, I trust that some schemes will be evolved that will bring to those parts of the country that have not shared as yet in increased industrial activity the benefits that other parts of the country are enjoying, where men and women have returned to work after years of misery and unemployment...

What of the health of the political life of the country? I think we are all aware of symptoms of intolerance that may tend to undermine our free political institutions. Action that is deliberately provocative and organised barracking are not compatible with British ideas of the free expression of opinion, and I am sure that not only hon Members in this House but the vast majority of the electorate will welcome with thankfulness and relief the assurance that a Bill is to be introduced to give power 'to deal more effectively with persons or organisations who provoke or cause disturbance of the public peace'. My hon Friend who is to second the Address will deal with those passages in the Gracious Speech which refer to international relationships, but I feel that I cannot sit down without a

The suffering comes from the knowledge that the fighting forces are not properly equipped and that human lives are being sacrificed because due preparation was neglected.

brief reference to a subject which is uppermost in our minds at present. I remain a convinced supporter of the policy of adherence to the League of Nations, and I am glad that the Government have made suggestions for the better working of such a body. The men and women of Great Britain are passionately anxious to maintain peace, and they are thankful that the Government have kept them out of entanglements that might lead to war. There is no diversity of opinion between men and women on the subject of peace, but in war time there comes a distinct cleavage between the burdens of suffering each is called upon to bear.

There are no scales whereby we can balance up the sum of human suffering, but I believe I speak for the women of Great Britain when I say that if ever the time comes again when women wait and men fight, there is one form of suffering they demand that they shall not have to undergo, and that is the suffering that comes from the knowledge that the fighting forces are not properly equipped and that human lives are being sacrificed because due preparation was neglected. A strong Britain, strong not only in her defence forces to deter aggression, but with her strength founded on the wellbeing of the individual and the mutual responsibility of her people can, I believe, bring to a world that is restless and almost despairing a real measure of hope and faith.

Talk to me about fairness, about decency, about equality! You are setting aside your laws for a rich, pampered Royalty.

George Buchanan
1890–1955

SPEECH DURING DEBATE ON ABDICATION BILL • HOUSE OF COMMONS
10 DECEMBER 1936

Whether it was a Conservative, Labour, or National government, George Buchanan was a persistent, and often violent, voice of protest. Early on in his Parliamentary career he was suspended from the House of Commons for calling a Tory MP who supported health cuts a 'murderer'. He was also an irritant to the Labour benches, although in 1935 he managed to get re-elected in the Gorbals despite facing an official Labour Party candidate.

George Buchanan was born in the Gorbals, the constituency he would later represent as an MP. He worked in a newspaper office before entering an apprenticeship as an engineer's patternmaker, and also joined the ILP. He was the youngest ever Glasgow town councillor and in 1922 was elected to Parliament. Having resisted ministerial office in the 1920s and '30s, Buchanan became a junior minister at the Scottish Office in 1945 and, from 1947, Minister for Pensions.

Described in the 1930s as 'the physical embodiment of… the poor but honest workman of the Gorbals',[23] with his dishevelled hair, broad physique, large face, booming voice and pugnacious manner, it was a role he was perfectly suited to. Buchanan had a deserved reputation for being irreconcilable in his political principles.

This speech is from the Commons debate on the abdication of King Edward III, which captured the world's imagination towards the end of 1936. Buchanan's contribution was the penultimate speech of the day and his frustration is clear. Short, sharp and to the point, he took an uncompromisingly anti-monarchist stance, and linked it to an attack on the working-class poverty he had highlighted throughout his career.

I FEEL THAT I OUGHT to express my own view and go a step farther than my hon Friend the Member for Bridgeton [Mr Maxton]. I should not be honest if I did not do so. I have listened to more cant and humbug than I have ever listened to in my life. I have heard praise of the King which was not felt sincerely in any quarter of the House. I go further. Who has not heard the tittle-tattle and gossip that is going about? If he had not voluntarily stepped from the Throne, everyone knows that the same people in the House who pay lip service to him would have poured out scorn, abuse and filth. Some months ago we opposed the Civil List. Tomorrow we shall take the same line. I have no doubt that you will go on praising the next King as you have praised this one. You will go on telling about his wonderful qualities. If he is a tenth as good as you say, why are you not keeping him? Why is everyone wanting to unload him? Because you know he is a weak creature. You want to get rid of him and you are taking the step today.

I have heard praise of the King which was not felt sincerely in any quarter of the House.

The great tragedy of it is this: If an ordinary workman had been in this mess, everyone in the House of Commons would have been ashamed of him. You would have refused him benefit. You would have ill-treated him. Look at the Minister of Labour sneering at collusive action. (Hon members: 'No, no!') Everyone knows it. The whole Law Courts were set at defiance for this man. A divorce case was taken when every one of you knows it was a breaking of the law. What are you talking nonsense about? The law is desecrated. The law courts are thrust aside. There is an association which everyone of you knows is collusive action. If a little boy in Wales leaves his mother to get 7s extra, he has to stand the jeers and taunts of a miserable Minister of Labour. Talk to me about fairness, about decency, about equality! You are setting aside your laws for a rich, pampered Royalty. The next set will be pampered too. You will lie and praise them and try to laud them above ordinary men. Instead of having the ordinary frailties that all of us have, they will have this additional one, of being surrounded with a set of flunkeys who refuse to let them know the truth as others do. Tomorrow I will willingly take the step of going out and saying it is time the people ceased to trust those folk, but only trusted their own power and their own elected authority.

We may yet save ourselves by our exertions, and democracy by our example.

Sir Archibald Sinclair
1890–1970

SPEECH DURING DEBATE ON PRIME MINISTER'S STATEMENT
HOUSE OF COMMONS

3 OCTOBER 1938

From 1935 the crisis in Europe dominated the British political agenda. While the governments of Stanley Baldwin and Neville Chamberlain pursued a policy of what became known as 'appeasement', piecemeal concessions to Mussolini and Hitler, the Labour Party maintained a high moral stance of opposition to fascism while rejecting the need for rearmament.

Archibald Henry Macdonald Sinclair, 1st Viscount Thurso, was born in 1890. After Eton and Sandhurst, Sinclair joined the army, where he became Winston Churchill's ADC during the First World War. In 1922 he entered Parliament himself as the MP for Caithness and Sutherland, becoming Scottish Secretary in 1931, Liberal leader in 1935 and Secretary of State for Air under Churchill in 1940. Sinclair joined the House of Lords in 1952 and died in 1970.

The Liberals, meanwhile, pursued a middle way, supporting collective security via the League of Nations while pushing for stronger defences. Sir Archibald Sinclair, a dashing Highland Scot who had formed a deep friendship with Winston Churchill during the First World War, was the Liberal leader. In the House of Commons he worked closely with Churchill to convince MPs of the need to prepare for war against Germany.

This speech is from the debate on the Munich Agreement, under which Chamberlain believed he had secured 'peace in our time' from the German Chancellor Adolf Hitler. In it, Sir Archibald patiently highlights all the inconsistencies in the Prime Minister's statement to that effect, while imploring MPs on all sides of the House to change tack before it was too late.

THE PRIME MINISTER asked us to accept two assurances which he has received from Herr Hitler. The first is that Herr Hitler has no wish to include in the Reich people of other races than the German. Yet, in the same speech in which the Prime Minister conveyed to Parliament that assurance from Herr Hitler, the Prime Minister told us that he had been informed by Herr Hitler that in his Bad Godesberg proposal he had offered to Czechoslovakia – I quote the Prime Minister's words: 'A frontier very different from the one he would have taken as the result of military conquest.' How does the Prime Minister reconcile those two very obviously contradictory statements? The second assurance was that this was the last of Herr Hitler's territorial ambitions in Europe. It is an ungrateful task to me, and an unusual task, to throw doubt on assurances formally given by the leading representative of a great Power, but it is useless to pretend to forget the assurances given by Herr Hitler after the re-occupation of the Rhineland... I have read the declaration which was signed by the Prime Minister and Herr Hitler, and I have listened to the Prime Minister's exposition of it, but I am left wondering still whether there is any real meaning and content in it. If there is, is it consistent with the Covenant of the League [of Nations]? I remember a speech by the Prime Minister in this House on 14 March in which he exhorted us to rely on a similar assurance which the German Government had

To our generation it falls to guard that flame.

given. The Prime Minister said then: 'I am informed that Field-Marshal Goering on 11 March gave a general assurance to the Czech Minister in Berlin – an assurance which he expressly renewed later on behalf of Herr Hitler – that it would be the earnest endeavour of the German Government to improve German-Czech relations.' I agree with the Prime Minister that we must weigh carefully the Chancellor's words, but not only one set of comforting words; we must weigh all his words together. Two sources of enlightenment I enjoy about Herr Hitler's intentions. One source is his public speeches and the expression of his opinions and intentions in public and in private, and the other is *Mein Kampf*. I prefer *Mein Kampf*, because it has never yet let me down, and I commend it to the Prime Minister.

The Prime Minister says that the Agreement in Munich is only the prelude to a larger settlement in which all Europe will find peace, but on what terms? On terms of German hegemony in Europe, or on terms of freedom? Months ago the League of Nations was already so much weakened that we were back into power-politics, and now the balance of power in Europe is disastrously dislocated. Thirty divisions which were held on the Czech frontier are now released and are available to be hurled against the Western frontier. The 12 Austrian divisions which Herr Hitler gained by the Anschluss are gradually being re-equipped and will be available next year in addition to the 30 divisions. No peace can last in the present state of the world unless it is buttressed by power, but when the Prime Minister talks of the necessity for our rearmament how can our rearmament keep pace with rearmament at the rate at which it is

The balance of power is Europe is disastrously dislocated.

going on in Germany? There are 40 divisions brought into the scale within a single year, and the resources of all the smaller States of the Near East of Europe are lying open to her exploitation.

A great national and international effort will be necessary if we are to preserve freedom in the world. Freedom and democracy are gravely threatened. Is the consultation that Herr Hitler has promised us in his Agreement with the Prime Minister to be like the consultations at Berchtesgaden and Bad Godesberg, the delivery of ultimatums? As the right hon Member for the St George's Division of Westminster said, they led to no good. It was only when the Government issued a

We must weigh all his words together.

statement that France and Russia and Britain were going to stand together, and when the ex-First Lord of the Admiralty mobilised the Fleet, that at last we got some concession upon the Godesberg terms from Herr Hitler. Let us have this peace conference of which the Leader of the Opposition talks. Let us hope that Germany and Italy will return to the League, and that we may once again be able to settle the affairs of the world through the League; but before that happens we shall have to make a great effort to preserve the essential foundations of freedom and order in the world, to preserve democracy, that form of government which is inspired by consciousness of the dignity of man and the use of power only for good and lawful ends. To our generation it falls to guard that flame. Let His Majesty's Government call upon the men and women of this country to rally to the defence of freedom and justice, and we may yet save ourselves by our exertions, and democracy by our example.

My one aim is to extirpate Hitlerism from Europe.

Winston Churchill
1874–1965

SPEECH AT GLASGOW CITY CHAMBERS

17 JANUARY 1941

At the beginning of 1941 Britain still fought on alone in the war against Hitler. On 17 January Harry Hopkins, the personal emissary of US President Roosevelt, visited Glasgow with Winston Churchill, the wartime Prime Minister. Their visit was supposed to be a secret but they arrived to discover a 'mob of hundreds if not thousands…waiting at Queen Street Station'.[24]

Battling their way to George Square, where the Prime Minister had been asked to say a few words to councillors and baillies at the city's opulent City Chambers, Hopkins and Churchill found 200 people, a platform and press reporters. 'The PM rose to the occasion however,' recorded Churchill's private secretary Jock Colville in his diary, 'though he had no prepared speech, and made a full length oration, which went down very well.'

Sir Winston Leonard Spencer Churchill was educated at Harrow and Sandhurst and after a brief Army and newspaper career was elected to Parliament in 1900. He held many posts in Liberal and Conservative governments until the early 1930s, and became Prime Minister in 1940. Churchill became premier again in 1951 but resigned four years later. He died in 1965.

I CAN HOLD OUT NO hopes of an easy passage. Before us lie dangers – I hardly like to say as great as those through which we have passed, but, at any rate, dangers which, if we neglect anything, might be fatal, mortal. Before us lie many months of having to endure bombardment of our cities and industrial areas without the power to make equal reply. Before us lie sufferings and tribulations. I am not one of those who pretend that smooth courses are open to us or that our experiences during this year are going to be deprived of terrible characteristics.

But what the end will be – about that I cannot have the slightest doubt. The two dictators are always endeavouring to feed their people with every kind of optimistic tale, but here we have made up our minds; here we look at facts with unillusioned eyes, because we are conscious of the rightness of our cause and because we are determined at this turning point in its fortunes.

Mr Harry Hopkins has come in order to put himself in the closest relation with things here. He will soon return to report to his famous chief the impressions he has gathered in our islands. We do not require in 1941 large armies from oversea[s]. What we do require are weapons, ships, and aeroplanes.

All that we can pay for we will pay for, but we require far more than we shall be able to pay for. And I watch with deep emotion the stirring processes by which the Democracy of the Great American Republic is establishing its laws and formulating its decisions in order to make sure that the British Commonwealth

Victory itself will only be a stimulus to further efforts to conquer ourselves and to make our country as worthy in the days of peace as it is proving itself in the hours of war.

of Nations is able to maintain, as it is maintaining at the present time, the front line of civilization and of progress.

My one aim is to extirpate Hitlerism from Europe. The question is such a simple one. Are we to move steadily forward and have freedom, or are we to be put back into the Middle Ages by a totalitarian system that crushes all forms of individual life and has for its aim little less than the subjugation of Europe and little more than the gratification of gangster appetites?

Do not suppose that we are at the end of the road. Yet, though long and hard it may be, I have absolutely no doubt that we shall win a complete and decisive victory over the forces of evil, and that victory itself will be only a stimulus to further efforts to conquer ourselves and to make our country as worthy in the days of peace as it is proving itself in the hours of war.

*I should like before I go from this place
to offer some of the amenities of life
to the peasant, his wife, and his family.*

Thomas Johnston
1881–1965

SPEECH DURING DEBATE ON HYDRO-ELECTRIC DEVELOPMENT
(SCOTLAND) BILL · HOUSE OF COMMONS

24 FEBRUARY 1943

In the first two years of the Second World War Thomas Johnston, already a veteran figure in Scottish public life, was keen to retire from party politics. So it was with some difficulty that Winston Churchill persuaded him to become Secretary of State for Scotland in February 1941. In a smart strategic move, Johnston agreed on the basis that he could form a 'Council of State' comprising all surviving Scottish Secretaries, and that anything agreed by them had to be accepted by the Cabinet.

Churchill agreed and selflessly, Johnston declined any ministerial salary. Although studies of the Council of State suggest its work was more symbolic than tangible, as a device it allowed Johnston to exploit the peculiar circumstances of wartime to reach broad agreement on political issues that had hitherto been subject to party political divisions. Chief among these was a long-touted scheme to bring electricity to the Highlands of Scotland by harnessing the natural power of water.

Thomas Johnston was born in Kirkintilloch in 1881 and educated at Lenzie Academy. After a spell in an insurance office he joined the ILP and established a newspaper – Forward – after inheriting a printing press, and edited that title even after entering Parliament in 1922. In 1929 Johnston became an undersecretary at the Scottish Office, and in 1941 Secretary of State for Scotland. He died in 1965.

This was perhaps Johnston's most enduring achievement, even if the North of Scotland Hydro-Electric Board did not quite have the transformative social effect he hoped it would (the Tennessee Valley Authority in the United States had been the model in this respect). In this speech, moving the Second Reading of the Hydro-Electric Development (Scotland) Bill, Johnston's vision is clear, as is his scorn for opponents of the scheme. Later, once he had finally retired from politics in 1945, Johnston would become chairman of the Hydro-Electric Board he had helped create.

EVERYBODY IS FOR amenity these days, and I am glad of it. The preservation of the beauty spots of Scotland is common form. But, occasionally, I could fain wish that some of the people who clamour for the preservation of amenities would remember that there are amenities other than landscape ones. For the people who live in the grandeur and the majesty of the Highlands, we could wish – some of us – that the definition of the word was widened and made more comprehensive. To some people, I gather, amenity means the provision of bathrooms in hotels marked by four stars in the automobile guide books, with a few poverty-stricken natives living in squalor amid picturesque reservations, much as the disappearing red races live in some parts of America. The cruisie and the farthing dip are no doubt quaint and interesting survivals, especially to summer visitors, but as lighting equipment their place is in a museum of antiquities. For my part, I should like before I go from this place to offer some of the amenities of life to the peasant, his wife, and his family. The amenities and comforts of civilisation have largely passed by the class from which Robert Burns sprang...

> To some people, I gather,
> amenity means the provision of bathrooms in
> hotels marked by four stars in the automobile guide books.

I will join with anybody in preventing Franco signs advertising somebody's beer or soap on the mountain-side at Sligachan, but my idea of amenity is not that it should begin about 12th August and last only until the deer stalking and salmon fishing seasons are over. And the chief amenity I should like to see carried into the life of the North of Scotland is the amenity of social security, the right to work and the amenity which derives from remuneration for a useful service in the world. Here in this Bill, directly and indirectly, is some contribution to that end. But there need be and there ought to be no disfigurement or desecration of our beautiful scenery, either by the hydro works or by industries which we hope will be attracted to the Highlands. Many hon Members no doubt have seen with what artistry even a modern pithead can be blended in the landscape at the Comrie pit in Fife, where the Fife Coal Company have shown other industrialists an example. It is as far removed from the old hideous pithead monstrosities as day is from night, and even the ranks of artistic Tuscany can scarce forbear to cheer when they visit Comrie and see neither dirt nor disorder nor, if I may coin the word, uglification of the countryside...

We do not say that the Bill as it stands in every Clause and to the last comma of it is perfect. In the language of the *Book of Common Prayer*, we would avoid: the two extremes of too much stiffness in refusing and of too much easiness in admitting any variation. But by the general principles of the Bill we stand. We believe the application of these principles is the first step in planning for the regeneration of the Highlands of Scotland. The Bill will give considerable employment, direct and indirect, in coal, iron, steel, cable-making, electrical engineering, cement, house and civil building works, and contracting. On the basis of the experience of the Central Electricity Board the operations of the Board on an expenditure of £30,000,000 should give employment, direct and indirect, of the order of 10,000 men for a number of years. In its train the Bill will bring a better placing and location of industry. It will provide amenities for the Highland population which will otherwise be denied them. I commend the Bill to the House, as I believe it has already commended itself to the vast majority of people in the country.

Do we want education
to breed a race of docile North Britons?

Robert McIntyre
1913–1998

MAIDEN SPEECH • HOUSE OF COMMONS

1 MAY 1945

By the Second World War Robert McIntyre had become disillusioned with the Labour Party's failure to deliver Home Rule for Scotland and instead joined the Scottish National Party. As the SNP's membership secretary from 1940, he set about revitalizing the party's organisation and electoral strategy. This paid dividends in 1944, when Douglas Young narrowly lost the Kirkcaldy by-election.

Robert Douglas McIntyre was born near Motherwell in 1913, a son of the manse. He was educated at Hamilton Academy, Daniel Stewart's College, and studied medicine at the universities of Edinburgh and Glasgow. McIntyre joined the Labour Party in 1936 but later defected to the SNP, becoming its first MP in 1945 and chairman from 1948–56. He also served as provost of Stirling from 1967–75, and died in 1998.

McIntyre also benefitted personally when, in April 1945, he beat the Labour candidate to become the SNP's first Member of Parliament following the Motherwell by-election. Arriving at the Commons, McIntyre initially refused to take sponsors upon his introduction as an MP. 'Next day he thought better of it and accepted sponsors,' recorded Harold Nicolson in his diary, 'but even then, as he reached the box, he said, "I do this under protest", which was not liked at all. He is going to be a sad nuisance and pose as a martyr.'[25]

McIntyre was an MP for just 21 days (a general election followed soon after) and his maiden speech came during a debate on Scottish Education on 1 May 1945. Although by no means an outstanding speech it is undoubtedly historically important.

IN RISING TO SPEAK here for the first time, I would hope for the consideration which I understand is customary. Also I might state that I am in a rather singular position – not only numerically – for I, and the colleagues who will shortly follow me from Scotland, come here with no intention of interfering in the affairs of this country or reforming any of the legislation, or of changing any of the customs of this House. We come with the intention of returning as soon as possible to our own country, where we may, under democratic government, achieve the long-needed reconstruction of Scotland. In the meantime... it is necessary for us to do everything in our power to safeguard the Scottish position from any further deterioration...

Before a new road is made, it is advisable to know just where it is leading. In Scotland, you can have either a Scottish education, or an education which is a poor imitation and copy of the English product... Scottish education has a different fundamental social basis from any English education...

In Scotland,
you can have either a Scottish education,
or an education which is a poor imitation
and copy of the English product.

The fundamental basis of Scottish education has always been a democratic one. On the other hand, the basis of English education, it appears to me as an outsider, is of the nature of a caste basis and an anti-democratic or feudal basis. These two cannot mix. They are like oil and water. They can, however, live side by side...

Is it the aim of education in Scotland to help raise Scottish citizens, or do we want education to breed a race of docile North Britons? I think that education should be for the citizenship of a democratic country and that it should not be for the fake citizenship of a slave State...

There is little to be said for bringing in this Bill at this time. It may be said that there are party considerations which make it necessary to introduce this

... I happen to be more interested in the
education and the welfare of the people of Scotland
than in any party consideration.

Bill just now, but I happen to be more interested in the education and the welfare of the people of Scotland than in any party consideration. We need a real programme for rebuilding our educational system in Scotland. We need a thorough-going measure of educational reform in Scotland. I hope the Secretary of State [of Scotland] will assist us in building up the only democratic body which can put through such a measure of reform in Scotland. I refer to a Scottish Parliament.

We consider that our light will be a beacon to those at the moment in totalitarian darkness and will give them a hope of return to freedom.

Sir David Maxwell Fyfe
1900–1967

SPEECH AT THE SIGNING OF THE
EUROPEAN CONVENTION ON HUMAN RIGHTS • ROME
4 NOVEMBER 1950

Shortly after the Universal Declaration of Human Rights was adopted in December 1948, it quickly became clear the next step, a legally binding charter, would take a number of years to achieve. A number of individuals seized the initiative to make faster progress at the European level where the differences between legal systems, which already respected fundamental rights, were ostensibly easier to reconcile. In this context, the Convention was forged on a ravaged continent where the memory of Nazi occupation was still fresh, and fear of Communist influence from the East was becoming more prevalent.

Sir David Maxwell Fyfe was born in Edinburgh in 1900 and later established himself as a barrister in Liverpool. Elected the Conservative MP for the city in 1935, he served as Solicitor and Attorney General in Winston Churchill's wartime administrations. Fyfe was the lead British prosecutor during the Nuremberg Trials and, when the Conservatives returned to office in 1951, Fyfe was appointed Home Secretary and latterly Lord Chancellor.

Sir David Maxwell Fyfe played a key role in the production of a draft Convention under the auspices of the pro-unity European Movement, which he then presented to the Council of Europe, established in 1949 to facilitate greater European co-operation. It was endorsed by that body's Consultative Assembly (with Fyfe as the chair of its legal committee) and referred to the executive Committee of Ministers who prepared their own draft during 1950. Ultimately, the final text was the result of many hands and not one but four committees, all of which struggled to reconcile competing legal traditions, ideologies, faiths and the prevailing political priorities of the day.

When the second draft was referred back to the Assembly, delegates expressed frustration at what they regarded as the Convention's emaciation. Led by Fyfe, a number of amendments were suggested, which were mostly rejected out of hand by the Committee of Ministers. As a result, the German and French Assembly delegates decided to boycott the signing ceremony in Rome on 4 November 1950.

Fyfe, however, was in a more compromising mood and made a short speech – safe in the knowledge that his role as one of the Convention's founding fathers was secure.

THE COUNCIL OF EUROPE has taken a definite step to carry out its aims by drawing up 'the rules of the Club'. It has laid down the minimum standards of human dignity and freedom compatible with membership. In some countries which have been fortunate enough not to lose individual human rights the matter may seem of small importance, but as the majority of our members have seen literally all human rights disappear in their own lands during the last ten years, the importance for them is obvious.

It will be observed that we have chosen simple rights. Indeed, it is a bitter commentary on the 20th century that almost all of them would have been taken for granted in almost every country in 1900.

> It has laid down the minimum standards of
> human dignity and freedom compatible with membership.

Anyone who has had to study the onset of totalitarians would agree that there is a tide in the affairs of states which, taken at the flood, sweeps on its people and leaves them high and dry on the rocks of tyranny. Nevertheless, there is always a moment when the guiding lights of democracy and reason, though burning low, are not extinguished. The problem is how these lights can be tended in time. We believe that an impartial and objective examination by an international body of the alleged infringements of a generally accepted code of individual freedoms would illuminate the dangers for all good democrats to see. We believe, further, that when the truth of the situation is seen, a stand against the encroachments of tyranny would be made.

Some may say that it is of doubtful value that the democratic nations should reinforce individual liberty among themselves and leave the totalitarian states untouched. We do not accept this pessimistic view. We consider that our light will be a beacon to those at the moment in totalitarian darkness and will give them a hope of return to freedom. Further, the Convention need not only be a test of membership, if it is adopted, but also a passport of return to our midst.

*Recent events have emphasised
that the Scottish still remember
their past and are still determined to
preserve their identity in the future.*

John MacCormick
1904–1961

RECTORIAL ADDRESS • ST ANDREW'S HALL • UNIVERSITY OF GLASGOW

8 JANUARY 1951

John MacCormick, known as 'King John', was a talented orator and political organiser throughout the 1930s and '40s. The failure of the old National Party of Scotland to achieve electoral success led him to change tactics, and from the Second World War until his death he was the leading figure in several cross-party initiatives to pressure Westminster into devolving power to a Scottish Parliament in Edinburgh.

His election as Rector of Glasgow University in late 1950 was a recognition of MacCormick's relative fame, although he was never elected to Parliament. Shortly after his election, MacCormick became involved with the theft by some students of the Stone of Destiny from Westminster Abbey. So when he stood before students in St Andrew's Hall on the day of his installation, his audience was expecting fireworks.

John MacDonald MacCormick was born in Glasgow in 1904, the son of a sea captain. He studied law at the University of Glasgow and formed the Glasgow University Scottish Nationalist Association in 1927, to promote Scottish culture and self-government. Active in the early years of the SNP, in 1938 MacCormick launched the Scottish National Convention and, in 1951, the Scottish Covenant Association. He failed to be elected as a Liberal at the 1959 general election and died two years later.

Unusually for a Rectorial address, MacCormick was given a 'cordial' hearing and two 'tumultuous ovations', one at the beginning and another at the end of his 45-minute speech. The political content is interesting, and reflects the fact that MacCormick was not a dogmatic politician, describing himself as a radical, by which he meant a sort of centrist Liberal (and indeed he later stood for election as a Liberal candidate). He attacks an over-centralised State, and warns that it may compromise greater freedoms.

THE AGE WHICH was to have become, and might well have become, the age of plenty and of freedom, has become the age of candlelight, of rations, of restrictions, of controls. Not in one nation only, not even in one-sixth of the world only, but everywhere men have accepted as inevitable that their fates lie in other hands than their own.

The Welfare State has become not a means to an end, but the substitute as an ideal for the man of independent mind.

It was in that new context that we spoke about a planned economy in a planned society... and he disliked and distrusted those terms.

Who was to be the architect of the plan? For what purposes was the plan conceived? He suspected that the half-conscious idea which lay in the minds of the planners was that ordinary men and women should leave themselves in the hands of experts who knew what we ought to want and would take care that that was all we could get.

We placed power into too few hands,
and that was the first long step on the road to disaster.

Foresight could not be blueprinted. Organisation was better than chaos; but the free spirit of man must always be ready to rebel against organisation and to create that disorder out of which a better order came.

One criticism of too much planning was that when it dealt with large societies it must deal in statistics. We could readily slip into the error of supposing we could discover a strange being whom we called the average man. There was no such creature. Yet every fully planned large-scale society was planned for the convenience of that non-existent average man.

That factor of differentiation amongst us, which was an inconvenience to planners and rulers, was surely something which we should wish to raise rather than to destroy. In a truly free society it should reach its maximum. Yet we had gone a long way towards its liquidation. It was a lamentable fact that in modern societies such methods as the Gallup Poll could accurately forecast public opinion.

We were so deeply bogged in purely material problems that we forgot to lift our eyes to the heights which were our goal. There were so many houses to be built, payments to be balanced, industries to be organised, that we had come to accept those things as ends in themselves.

We did not come into this world as citizens of the world.
We were born as members of a family.

There is no final human purpose in building houses if they are merely to be occupied by Helots. There is no use providing a national health service if it is only to perpetuate a race of slaves.

We had to seek freedom first and all other things would be added to it. If we forgot freedom we should fall into error, and we had already fallen into the most grievous error of all. We had placed too much power into too few hands, and that was the first long step on the road to disaster.

Our present party differences were often not in any true sense political differences at all. They were too often mere disputes as to who should have the right to award jobs for the boys. His own protest was not because he did not like any particular set of politicians, but because he knew that any concentration of power was dangerous to human freedom.

In a State which had grown too large, and whose affairs had become too complex, the dead weight of necessary organisation would stifle enterprise, initiative, and daring, and would therefore, in the long run, bring economic disaster.

> ... the free spirit of man must always be ready
> to rebel against organisation and to create disorder
> out of which a better order came.

But what was worse than economic disaster, it would destroy the sense of freedom in the ordinary man. The State became for him something infinitely remote and infinitely mysterious, as inscrutable and as inexorable in its ways as any juggernaut.

It was therefore good sense as well as sound idealism to devolve the powers of government. We should aim to the utmost reasonable extent at restricting the area in which the powers of the State were to be exercised.

Recent events have emphasised that the Scottish still remember their past and are still determined to preserve their identity in the future. But one thing should be added. We face dangers from outside as well as from within. It becomes a specious argument, therefore, to say that at all costs unity must be maintained.

We did not come into the world as citizens of this world. We were born as members of a family. From the natural groupings of family with family, clan with clan, nation with nation, the full adult knowledge of still wider unities arose. They were the stepping-stones to world citizenship, and, if they were submerged, humanity would not be united, but destroyed.

Somebody is minded now to introduce sponsored broadcasting into this country.

John Reith
1889–1971

SPEECH DURING DEBATE ON BROADCASTING POLICY • HOUSE OF LORDS

22 MAY 1952

In 1952, the Conservative government led by the ageing war leader Winston Churchill published a white paper setting out its plans for a system of commercial television which would break the BBC's monopoly. As one of the Corporation's founding fathers and stoutest defenders, John Reith was appalled that his concept of broadcasting as a way of educating the masses was under threat from what many regarded as the inevitably 'vulgar' transmissions of 'sponsored' television.

A member of the House of Lords since the Second World War, Reith led the attack on the white paper from the Opposition despatch box. He had worked on his speech all night, and its sermon-like tone reflected Reith's Kirk background. 'The speech of the debate was Lord Reith's,' wrote the Parliamentary correspondent of the *Manchester Guardian*. 'Nothing quite like it has been heard in the House of Lords. It was more like the utterance of a prophet, and it was clear from the faces on the Government front bench that prophets are an embarrassment to them.'[26]

Embarrassed, but undeterred, the government pressed ahead with its plans and in 1954 the Independent Television Authority was established, from which emerged ITV, finally breaking the BBC's monopoly.

Lord Reith's life was, according to his biographer Ian McIntyre, a 'classical tragedy... of baroque proportions'. He founded, and for its first 16 years directed, the BBC, establishing a model of public service broadcasting copied all over the world. Born in Stonehaven, Kincardineshire, in 1889, Reith's father was a minister of the United Free Church of Scotland, and those austere Presbyterian values governed his whole life and career. After being persuaded to step down as the BBC's director-general in 1938, Reith tried ,but failed, to find another job to absorb his prodigious talents and energies.

M Y LORDS, I HAVE left till last the most serious point of all; one that is not concerned with administration or with the Corporation as such, but with broadcasting itself – its worth and consequence, the flower and essence. The White Paper says: ... 'that in the expanding field of television provision should be made to permit some element of competition.' Now either that is a complete non sequitur, or else the Government do not appreciate the significance of television. There is nothing hypothetical about television. Its effect, even under responsible control, presents, I suppose, one of the gravest, most critical and most baffling social problems of the day. Both by the nature of television and the nature of the audience, nothing could be more certain than that Gresham's Law will apply and dominate, far more in television than in sound broadcasting.

> British broadcasting...
> an institution of which England – yes,
> and Scotland and Wales and Northern Ireland – can be proud.

There is no mention of sponsoring in the whole Paper; but the income guarantee to the BBC means that any competitor will have to finance himself. And is that likely to any extent or for any time, otherwise than by sponsoring? Have the Government any other means in mind? If not, why is sponsoring not mentioned? ...

I have never spoken on broadcasting in this House before. I may have done this great cause no good: maybe even harm, because I well realise that, during the years of my association with the BBC, I built up for myself an immense unpopularity and dislike which surrounds me still. And yet what was done was approved. For that I claim no credit. I tried to do as I had been taught in the Manse of the College Church in Glasgow. I believe that I was peculiarly helped in plan and execution, and through every sort of opposition, vehement and powerful and determined though it often were. To-day, thanks to Sir William Haley [the then director-general of the BBC], and Governors, and a devoted staff, British broadcasting commands the respect and admiration of the whole world;

> There is nothing hypothetical about television.
> Its effect... presents, I suppose, one of the gravest,
> most critical and baffling social problems of the day.

an institution of which England – yes, and Scotland and Wales and Northern Ireland – can be proud; one which we should be jealous and quick to safeguard and defend.

What grounds are there for jeopardising this heritage and tradition? Not a single one is even suggested in the White Paper. Why sell it down the river?

Do we find leadership and decision in this White Paper; or compromise and expediency – a facing-both-ways? A principle absolutely fundamental and cherished is scheduled to be scuttled. It is the principle that matters, and it is neither here nor there that the scuttling may not take place for years. The Government are here on record to scuttle – a betrayal and a surrender; that is what is so shocking and serious; so unnecessary and wrong. Somebody introduced dog-racing into England; we know who, for he is proud of it, and proclaims it *urbi et orbi* ['to the City of Rome and to the World'] in the columns

> I ask the Government... to think again.

of *Who's Who*. And somebody introduced Christianity and printing and the uses of electricity. And somebody introduced smallpox, bubonic plague and the Black Death. Somebody is minded now to introduce sponsored broadcasting into this country. 'Two things' said Immanuel Kant, 'fill the mind with wonder and awe, the more often and the more intently the mind of thought is drawn to them – the starry heavens above me, the moral law within me.' The stars are somewhat depreciated, and man is losing his sense of wonder in these egalitarian days. But what about the moral law? Need we be ashamed of moral values, or of intellectual and ethical objectives? It is these that are here and now at stake. My powers of persuasion may be feeble, my influence very slight, but with all the earnest and urgent conviction of which a man is capable. I ask the Government... to think again. I appeal to them to do so. And leave this thought with them, 'because right is right, to follow right were wisdom in the scorn of consequence.

Homosexuality is far more prevalent in this country than is generally admitted.

Robert Boothby
1900–1986

SPEECH TO THE HARDWICKE SOCIETY
MIDDLE TEMPLE COMMITTEE ROOM • LONDON
19 FEBRUARY 1954

B y the mid-1950s, Robert Boothby's political career was more or less over. A talented minister in the 1930s, when Winston Churchill returned to office in 1951 there was no post for Boothby. Instead, he was appointed KBE in 1953 and his numerous appearances on television and radio programmes – for Boothby was engaging and articulate – made him a household name.

Robert 'Bob' John Graham Boothby, Baron Boothby, was born in Edinburgh in 1900, the only child of a banker. He was educated at Eton and Magdalen College, Oxford, and entered Parliament shortly after graduating in 1924. He held East Aberdeenshire for nearly 34 years, became Churchill's PPS in 1926 and an under-secretary at the Ministry of Food during the Second World War. Boothby became one of the first life peers in 1958, published several books and died of a heart attack in 1986.

Boothby was also, although this did not emerge until much later, actively bisexual. That is the crucial context to this important speech, although one which all but the best-informed members of Boothby's audience would have been unaware. Boothby's argument is a subtle one, and the speech apparently led to a correspondence between him and the then Home Secretary, Sir David Maxwell Fyfe, which in turn resulted in the appointment of the Wolfenden Committee.

In a postscript to the speech published in one of his many books, Boothby predicted that Wolfenden had altered the 'climate of opinion' and that, in time, 'some private Member of Parliament or, better still, some private Lord' would introduce a measure to change the law and that it would 'be passed… in an empty House on a hot August night, without discussion and without a division. And the job will have been done.'[27] It was, just five years after Boothby wrote those words, although not in Scotland.

L ET ME START WITH a sweeping assertion, which I claim cannot be denied. Homosexuality is far more prevalent in this country than is generally admitted. It is increasing steadily, and it is by no means confined to the metropolis. There is, in fact, a homosexual 'underground' in most of our large provincial cities of disturbing dimensions, which is a continuous menace to youth. We have reached a situation in which no man with any regard for his reputation will dare to enter a public urinal after dark; and in which the number of male prostitutes parading our streets is a by-word in every other country, and a disgrace to our own.

For this the innate hypocrisy of the British people on all matters concerning sex is largely responsible. It is a hang-over from the Victorian Age. Unless and until it is forced upon our attention by the activities of the police, we shut our eyes to the existence of the problem.

> What consenting adults do in privacy may be a
> moral issue between them and their Maker:
> but is certainly not a legal issue between them and the State...

Those who are revolted by the whole subject are the worst offenders. Instead of facing up to it they shroud it in a veil of secrecy, silence and shame. As for the police, their sporadic campaigns against homosexuality, which are often accompanied by methods of great dubiety, do nothing towards its eradication. On the contrary they intensify the squalor by which it is surrounded, and widen the areas in which the underground flourishes...

The present laws governing the treatment of homosexual offences in this country are sections 61 and 62 of the Offences against the Person Act of 1861, and section 11 of the Criminal Law Amendment Act of 1886. Both were passed long before the discoveries of modern psychology; and, in my submission, they are no deterrent to the practice of homosexuality...

[Section 11 of the Criminal Law Amendment Act of 1886] introduced the horrifying elements of tainted evidence and blackmail into a situation which was already sufficiently dark and difficult; and the sooner it is repealed the better.

> Those who are revolted
> by the whole subject are the worst offenders.

In cases involving alleged acts of indecency committed in private, where there is no injured party, the witnesses are almost invariably accomplices, actuated by motives of hatred, avarice, jealousy or fear. These emotions lie at the root of all evil, and have made the field of homosexuality a happy hunting-ground for the blackmailer...

I conclude from this that the existing laws dealing with the matter are outmoded – and indeed medieval. By attaching so fearful a stigma to homosexuality as such, they put a large number of otherwise law-abiding and useful citizens on the wrong side of the fence which divides the good citizen

The existing laws dealing with the matter are outmoded – and indeed medieval.

from the bad. By making them feel that, instead of being unfortunates they are social 'pariahs', they drive them into ineffable squalor – perhaps even into crime; and produce that underground movement which it is so clearly in the public interest to eradicate. Since the homosexual finds that an important part of the moral code is unworkable so far as he is concerned, he tends to question and reject other parts of that code; and to challenge both society and the State in other fields as well.

There is a sharp distinction to be drawn between conduct which may be held to be sinful and that which is criminal. The duty of the State, as I see it, is to protect youth from corruption and the public from indecency or nuisance. What consenting adults do in privacy may be a moral issue between them and their Maker: but is certainly not a legal issue between them and the State...

I am well aware that this is not a popular cause. The inhibitions on the part of the public and of Parliament are indeed daunting to anyone who espouses it. Nevertheless I believe that the magnitude of the problem, and the amount of avoidable suffering that is now being caused, demand that it should be faced. That is why I am asking for the appointment of a Royal Commission, or some similar authoritative Enquiry, to furnish Parliament with the expert knowledge and guidance which are necessary for appropriate legislative and administrative action.

I for one cannot press that button. Can you?

George MacLeod
1895–1991

SPEECH TO THE GENERAL ASSEMBLY OF THE CHURCH OF SCOTLAND,
EDINBURGH

MAY 1954

The 15 years following the Second World War were the great days of the Iona Community – an ecumenical Christian community, founded by George MacLeod, and thus the high point of his impressive career. It became regarded as one of the great selling points of the Church of Scotland to the global spiritual community. Although heavily involved, MacLeod also directed his significant energy to other matters.

One of the great preachers of his day, MacLeod's sermons, according to Duncan Forrester, 'invited people to encounter reality at a new depth, and challenged them to go and transform the world'. In May 1954, during one of the General Assembly of the Church of Scotland's great set-piece debates, MacLeod challenged his fellow ministers to do precisely that. A pacifist since the Second World War, he had regularly initiated almost ritualistic debates on that subject.

George Fielden MacLeod, Baron MacLeod of Fuinary, was born in 1895 to a political family. He was educated at Winchester College and Oriel College, Oxford, before enlisting in the Argyll and Sutherland Highlanders during the First World War. Thereafter he entered the Kirk ministry and founded the Iona Community in 1938.

This speech is from one such occasion. The packed Assembly was hushed as MacLeod argued that it was meaningless to ban the hydrogen bomb while justifying the atomic bomb. Someone, he said, had to call a halt. When it came to a vote, however, MacLeod was overwhelmingly defeated. Only in 1986 did the General Assembly adopt one of his motions, 'that no church can accede to the use of nuclear weapons to defend any cause whatever'.

WE ARE ALL COMMITTED either to press the button of the hydrogen bomb or to renounce it now. No one is going to leave the opprobrium of the pressing to some RAF lad, knowing that the man who pressed it for Hiroshima resigned his commission and is now in a monastery, and the only English observer also resigned and is looking after cripples...

You go down into that dark, seemingly grave-like valley that is called pacifism, a valley largely untrodden since the first three centuries of Christianity. When you first find yourself there, phantom serpents seem to be hissing at you, 'cowardice!' and imaginary beasts seem to be breathing in your face the word 'treason!' All the centuries-old traditions of Scotland and our fathers whisper around you and half of your best friends, if only by their silent eyes, seem to be saying, 'Mad! Mad! Mad!' and yet there is no halting place of sanity higher up.

The time is past when men can speak of war as an instrument of policy. Surely in such a plight the only people left who can give the releasing word are the people of God? For only they know the secret and significance of the grave. They alone know the paradoxical possibilities of resurrection. Only the Church of Jesus Christ can now release our world...

I for one cannot press that button. Can you?

He reigns omnipotent, and the destination of mankind is in his hands.

... The mind boggles, so we dismiss it because no one will ever dare drop it. But it is well within living memory that all the great nations refused the submarine, as making sea warfare too ungentlemanly. But the submarine came...

We pacifists have come to believe that in the strict sense that calculation is a worldly one. The pacifist solution is beyond peradventure a Christian calculation. It is that the Cross of Christ looked like the final victory of the powers of darkness. But it wasn't so. The calculation is that God does not abdicate. He reigns omnipotent, and the destination of mankind is in his hands.

The Parliament of Scotland which God has miraculously preserved for us for 250 years.

Wendy Wood
1892–1981

ADDRESS TO THE GENERAL ASSEMBLY
OF THE CHURCH OF SCOTLAND • EDINBURGH

30 MAY 1960

Wendy Wood was one of the most colourful figures produced by the early years of the Scottish Nationalist movement. A Home Rule Liberal in 1912, she joined the Scottish League in 1916, the Scottish Home Rule Association in 1918, and thereafter progressed through the National Party of Scotland and the SNP before forming her own organisation, the direct-action Scottish Patriots. Wood later claimed to have experienced a Nationalist epiphany at the Wallace Monument in 1913.

Wood likened herself to a Scottish version of Maud Gonne, 'the queen of demagogues',[28] raising Nationalist consciousness through energetic addresses at public meetings. With her piercing blue eyes and 'rugged, purposeful look',[29] Wood averaged 32 of these speeches a year and, in 1957, spoke at no fewer than 73. By the time Wood moved to Edinburgh in the late 1950s, her political activities had entered a new phase.

She and the Scottish Patriots believed the old 'Scottish estates' that used to govern Scotland ought to be recalled and on 30 May 1960 Wood rose to address the General Assembly of the Church of Scotland with that argument. It was unusual for a woman to address the Assembly on matters not connected with Church organisation, but it had an effect: the Kirk's Church and Nation Committee of the Kirk put forward a motion in support of Scottish Home Rule, and this was accepted by the following year's General Assembly.

Gwendoline Emily Meacham, also known as Wendy Wood, was born in Kent in 1892, the daughter of a scientist (her Scottish ancestry came via her mother). Growing up in South Africa, Wood initially flourished as an artist before becoming active in politics. She stood for election to Edinburgh town council in 1935 and at the Glasgow Bridgeton by-election in 1946, where she gained 14 per cent of the vote. A talented storyteller in later life, Wood died in 1981.

MODERATORS, FATHERS AND BRETHREN I feel very conscious of the honour that is done me in permitting me to come reverently and with great hope to the Bar of this Assembly... nearly all the questions that are rightly troubling the conscience of the men of God's Kirk of Scotland, nearly all these troubles can be eliminated by the recurring of the Scottish Parliament, which still exists, to walk back into its House and to proclaim a general action for Scotland.

Might I remind you you have been discussing very many things, and particularly housing... Moderator, we do not need earthquakes in Scotland for our houses to come down, they come down without it, but it is a disgrace to our country and our Church that we should have the worst slums in the whole of Europe... The Church knows full well if we had our own Parliament sitting again that housing is one of the first things that would be undertaken...

You wonder at the criminal figures of youth in Scotland; you are not attracting youth in the Church. Why? I think – without in the least meaning to be personal

We have been denationalised of our Scottish qualities... that used to be known throughout the world.

or impertinent – I would remind you that looking down from the galleries of this house we are looking down on heads as grey as my own, some of them whose particular colour of hair one could not exactly say, but nevertheless one is not looking down upon a Church that has a youthful ministry, and that is part of the reason why youth is not in the Church, and the whole thing boils down to this, and that is a lack of vision, people without vision perish. Youth has got vision; old men dream dreams and young men see visions. There is the vision of a new Scotland with employment, with houses, and with a great spiritual uplift which I feel it is the duty of the Church of Scotland to consider and to provide for...

It is an appalling thing to have to face anybody and admit that Scotland has got low morale, that is the business of the Church of Christ in Scotland; you have been told how to cure it, do you not want to face it, what is the fear that is in you, why are you afraid before God to admit that a man who stands in a high position in Glasgow University, Professor Highet has said that the cure for low morale in

Youth has got vision; old men dream dreams and young men see visions.

Scotland is self-government? It is the business of the Church to raise the morale of our country. You know how the character of the Scots has gone down, you know how we have been Anglicised, we have been denationalised of our Scottish qualities of good craftsmanship, of integrity in character, of sturdy independence of character, of honesty that used to be known throughout the world. You know what men work for today, wages; they have to have them, yes, but the old craftsmanship and the old integrity has gone. This is one of the very few institutions that is Scottish in the country, and did they not try to go and give you bishops, even at that. I would ask you to realise in a very big newspaper which shall be nameless only this week this Assembly was alluded to as the Assembly of the Church of England. It has gone that far, and it is an extraordinary thing that it could happen, but it means that even the Assembly of the Church of Scotland is not associated in other countries with Scotland.

You have been speaking today of Kenya, of Nyasaland and of other countries in Africa, you are troubled about Nyasaland, and similarly, you must see the necessity for our own land of Scotland to have the power of government, to be able to protect our character and our ideals. It seems to me that you want this for Nyasaland, that you want that for Nyasaland, that you want independence for Bechuanaland, that you are congratulating Nigeria on having obtained

I can only pray that Almighty God will reveal to you the vision of the new Scotland...

independence, and we are your own people who sit in the seats in Church on Sunday, we are your own people powerless ourselves to relieve the troubles of our own people...

You have in this House during this week so rightly welcomed someone from Ghana; Ghana was brought to its position of independence by strife; what we are asking, we are pleading, we are craving that the Church of Scotland which has hitherto said that it is in sympathy with the demand for self-government for Scotland, we are asking that you should accept the key to the Parliament of Scotland which God has miraculously preserved for us for 250 years, the Parliament of Scotland is there today... Other countries have had to fight for the right to manage their affairs, God has put into our hands the miracle that our Parliament still remains and that all you are asked to do is that you approve the return of the Three Estates. I can only pray that Almighty God will reveal to you the vision of the new Scotland and will not connote a Church of Scotland to that vision of a country with new spirit rising, a country that may express its own conscience among the nations of the world, a conscience among the nations of the world, a conscience that may show that the spirit of Scotland is still for good and for the great ideals. It is no material thing that I am asking and I plead with you that this crave be permitted, that you give to Scotland the chance to bring to reality all the ideals which have been expressed in this House.

I am a teacher! I am a teacher, first, last, always!

Miss Jean Brodie

FICTIONAL

SPEECH ON HER SACKING

MARCIA BLAINE SCHOOL FOR GIRLS · EDINBURGH

NOVEL PUBLISHED IN 1961

The character of Miss Jean Brodie was based in part on Christina Kay, who had taught Muriel Spark for two years at James Gillespie's High School for Girls in Edinburgh. 'What filled our minds with wonder and made Christina Kay so memorable', wrote Spark, 'was the personal drama and poetry within which everything in her classroom happened.' Like Miss Brodie, Kay used to display posters of Renaissance art alongside those of Mussolini.

It was also Kay who encouraged the young Muriel Spark (then Muriel Camberg) to become a writer. Her most famous novel, *The Prime of Miss Jean Brodie*, was published in 1961 and turned into a celebrated film starring Maggie Smith eight years later. This speech – more a wounded outburst – takes place towards the end of the tale, when one of the 'set', Sandy, confronts Miss Brodie over her role in sending another girl, Mary, to take part in the Spanish Civil War, where she was killed. Sandy then betrays Brodie to Miss Mackay, the headmistress, who decides finally to be rid of Miss Brodie.

Muriel Spark was born in Edinburgh in 1918, but left Scotland aged 19 to marry in Southern Rhodesia. She returned to the UK in 1944, establishing herself in London as a poet and critic. By the late 1950s Spark had published a series of acclaimed novels including **The Comforters** *and* **Memento Mori.** **The Prime of Miss Jean Brodie** *turned her into an international celebrity, and until her death Spark lived first in New York and latterly Tuscany, where she died in 2006.*

I AM A TEACHER! I am a teacher, first, last, always! Do you imagine that for one instant I will let that be taken from me without a fight? I have dedicated, sacrificed my life to this profession. And I will not stand by like an inky little slacker and watch you rob me of it and for what? For what reason? For jealousy! Because I have the gift of claiming girls for my own. It is true I am a strong influence on my girls. I am proud of it! I influence them to be aware of all the possibilities of life... of beauty, honour, courage. I do not, Miss Mackay, influence them to look for slime where it does not exist! I am going. When my class convenes, my pupils will find me composed and prepared to reveal to them the succession of the Stuarts. And on Sunday, I will go to Cramond to visit Mr Lowther. We are accustomed, bachelor and spinster, to spend our Sundays

I influence them to be aware of all the possibilities of life... of beauty, honour, courage.

together in sailing and walking the beaches and in the pursuit of music. Mr Lowther is teaching me to play the mandolin. Good day, Miss Mackay.[30]

I intend to march my troops towards the sound of gunfire.

Jo Grimond
1913–1993

SPEECH TO LIBERAL ASSEMBLY • BRIGHTON

15 SEPTEMBER 1963

Under Jo Grimond's leadership, the Liberal Party achieved a remarkable run of by-election results. Although the 1959 general election returned just six Liberal MPs, the party's share of the vote more than doubled to 5.9 per cent. This appeared to indicate progress, and when Eric Lubbock sensationally won Orpington in a March 1962 by-election, it looked as if the Liberals were on the cusp of an electoral breakthrough after half a century in the wilderness.

Joseph 'Jo' Grimond, Baron Grimond, was born in St Andrews in 1913, the son of a jute manufacturer. He had a comfortable and stimulating childhood, and after Eton and Oriel College, Oxford, he became a barrister, entering Parliament as the MP for Orkney and Shetland after the war. Grimond succeeded Clement Davies as Liberal leader in 1956, and served for more than a decade. He went to the House of Lords in 1983 and died ten years later.

Indeed, a National Opinion Poll published shortly after Orpington showed the Liberals – albeit fleetingly – to be the most popular party in the country. For this Grimond could claim much of the credit. He was media friendly, charismatic and sufficiently patrician in style to make him an attractive alternative for disaffected Tories.

Grimond also worked hard to depict the Liberals as a dynamic and classless party, while floating the idea of a realignment of the left in British politics. His memorable speech to the Liberal Assembly in September 1963 drew on that philosophy together with recent events in Orpington, while looking ahead to a general election due in 1964. With expectations so high, Grimond had to make the speech of his life. He did not disappoint, likening himself to a military commander who would lead his troops 'towards the sound of gunfire'.

WE SHALL HAVE OVER 400 candidates in the field at the election. Our hat... is in the ring, but there are many people who are genuinely puzzled by the effect of the Liberal campaign. Some of them may still be tempted to vote Tory or even to join the Tory Party for the sake of keeping Labour out. I ask them to reflect on the fate of those who have done this over the last 40 years. There have been plenty of rats to leave the sinking ship, but the ship has gone on and the rats have sunk (Applause)...

The people of this country, as I have said, are entitled to have politicians who stand up and tell the people what they mean. They are entitled to have politics in which the parties stand for some principle and, without that, you will never have healthy politics in this country.

> There have been plenty of rats
> to leave the sinking ship,
> but the ship has gone on and the rats have sunk.

One thing is certain about this election. Great interest is going to be fixed on the number of votes cast for Liberal candidates and the number of candidates returned. Even if there is not a Liberal Government, the temper of whatever government there is going to be will be validly affected by the public support given to the Liberal Party. If you want an example of how effective a Liberal vote can be, only consider the result at Orpington. Not even the crackest shot in the Tory Party has ever bagged six Cabinet Ministers with one barrel! (Loud applause.)

If we return after the election with a solid block of Liberals in the House of Commons, even if we do not hold a majority, we shall be able to influence the whole thinking of the country and attitude of whatever party may be in power.

> Our Government, for too long,
> has pretended not to see what it does not like.

We have made it clear that we intend to use that influence. As the election approaches we shall not shirk the battle, nor shall we be diverted by the great volume of criticism which we hope will pour down upon us. (Applause.)

War, delegates war has always been a confused affair. In bygone days the commanders were taught that when in doubt they should march their troops towards the sound of gunfire. I intend to march my troops towards the sound of gunfire. (Loud applause.) Politics are a confused affair and the fog of political controversy can obscure many issues. But we will march towards the sound of the guns.

> It has put the telescope to its blind eye...
> so that it can say that there is no enemy in sight.

Our Government, for too long, has pretended not to see what it does not like. It has put the telescope to its blind eye in a very un-Nelsonian mood, so it can say that there is no enemy in sight. But, delegates, there are enemies, there are difficulties to be faced. There are decisions to be made. There is passion to be generated. The enemy is complacency and wrong values and inertia in the face of incompetence and injustice. It is against this enemy that we march. (Applause.) We are not alone. The reforms which we advocate are inexorably written into the future. We move with the great trends of this century. Other nations have rebuilt their institutions under the hard discipline of war. It is for Liberals to show that Britain, proud Britain, can do this as a free people without passing through the furnace of defeat. (Loud applause.)

So, dear Edinburgh students, this may well be the last time I address you… and I don't really care whether it means anything to you or not.

Malcolm Muggeridge
1903–1990

'ANOTHER KING' SERMON AT HIGH KIRK OF ST GILES' • EDINBURGH

14 JANUARY 1968

For most of his life the journalist, writer and television presenter Malcolm Muggeridge had been unhappy, tormented by a strong desire for women and drink. Aged around 60, he renounced drinking, meat-eating, smoking and casual sex and, in print and on television, became a formidable apologist for Christianity.

So when Muggeridge was elected Rector of Edinburgh University in 1966, he was already out of kilter with the student body he was supposed to represent. The final straw came when Anna Coote, editor of the campus newspaper *Student*, goaded Muggeridge into supporting the introduction of contraceptive pills at the University Health Service.

Due to give a sermon at St Giles' at the beginning of 1968, Muggeridge did not originally intend to announce his resignation as Rector, but got so caught up in his oratorical onslaught against what he called the Student Representative Council's obsession with 'pot and pills' that he inserted this dramatic piece of news at the last minute.

(Thomas) Malcolm Muggeridge was born in Croydon in 1903, the son of a Labour MP. He was educated at Selhurst Grammar School and Selwyn College, Cambridge, and toyed with entering the Anglican ministry taking a teaching post at the Union Christian College near Madras. Thereafter Muggeridge taught in Birmingham, then Cairo, where he also began working as a journalist, later moving into television. He died in 1990.

NOWADAYS WHEN I occasionally find myself in a pulpit – one of those bad habits one gets into in late middle age – and never, by the way, in a more famous pulpit than this one, I always have the same feeling as I look round as I do now at your faces; a deep, passionate longing to be able to say something memorable, to shed some light…

This year, at 65 years old, I move into the NTBR (Not To Be Resuscitated) bracket, when some high minded, highly skilled doctor will look me over and decide in his infinite wisdom and humanity whether I am worth keeping alive.

As I have said, I alternate between a sense of the utter absurdity of it all and a desire to get out of so nonsensical a world.

May I... consider for instance the situation in this ancient University, with which through the accident of election I find myself briefly associated. The students here in this University, as in other universities, are the ultimate

I occasionally find myself in a pulpit – one of those bad habits one gets into in late middle age.

beneficiaries under our welfare system. They are supposed to be the spearhead of progress, flattered and paid for by their admiring seniors, an élite who will happily and audaciously carry the torch of progress into the glorious future opening before them. Now, speaking for myself, there is practically nothing that they could do in a mood of rebelliousness or refusal to accept the ways and values of our run down, spiritually impoverished way of life for which I shouldn't feel some degree of sympathy or, at any rate, understanding, up to and including blowing up this magnificent edifice in which we are now assembled. Yet how infinitely sad; how, in a macabre sort of way, funny that the form their insubordination takes should be a demand for Pot and Pills, for the most tenth rate sort of escapism and self-indulgence ever known! It is one of those situations a social historian with a sense of humour will find very much to his taste. All is prepared for a marvellous release of youthful creativity; we await the great works of art, the high spirited venturing into new fields of perception and understanding – and what do we get? The resort of any old, slobbering debauchee anywhere in the world at any time – Dope and Bed.

The feeling aroused in me by this, I have to confess, is not so much disapproval as contempt, and this, as you may imagine, makes it difficult, in fact impossible, for me as Rector to fulfil my functions. Here, if I may, I should like to insert a brief word of personal explanation. I, as Rector, and Allan Frazer as my Assessor, find ourselves as you know responsible for passing on to the university authorities the views and requests of the student body as conveyed to us by their elected officers, and as set forth in their magazine *Student* for whose conduct they are responsible. Their request concerning the birth pill is as it happens highly distasteful to us, as we have not hesitated to let it be known. The view of the SRC officers as expressed by some of them, and not repudiated publicly by any of them, is that the Rector and his Assessor are bound not only to pass on but to

However else we may venture into the unknown it is not I assure you on the plastic wings of Playboy magazine.

recommend whatever the SRC may decide. This is a role which, in my opinion, no self-respecting Rector, or Assessor, could possibly countenance, and I have therefore asked the Principal to accept my resignation, as has my Assessor.

The ensuing Rectorial contest, when it takes place, will serve to show, as I hope, what calibre of candidate will come forward to contest the Rectorship on the terms laid down by the present SRC officers, and whether the views now put forward by them in fact enjoy the support of a majority of the students of Edinburgh University.

> They are supposed to be the spearhead of progress,
> flattered and paid for by their admiring seniors.

So, dear Edinburgh students, this may well be the last time I address you, and this is what I want to say – and I don't really care whether it means anything to you or not, whether you think there is anything in it or not. I want you to believe that this row I have had with your elected officers has nothing to do with any puritanical attitudes on my part. I have no belief in abstinence for abstinence's sake, no wish under any circumstances to check any fulfilment of your life and being. But I have to say to you this: that whatever life is or is not about, it is not to be expressed in terms of drug stupefaction and casual sexual relations. However else we may venture into the unknown it is not I assure you on the plastic wings of Playboy magazine or psychedelic fancies.

We would propose...
the creation of an elected Scottish
Assembly,
to sit in Scotland.

Edward Heath
1916–2005

SPEECH TO SCOTTISH CONSERVATIVE PARTY CONFERENCE • PERTH
18 MAY 1968

W innie Ewing's victory in the Hamilton by-election of November 1967 sent shockwaves through British politics. The Scottish National Party had won a sensational victory and the main UK parties, Labour and Conservative, felt compelled to respond. While Harold Wilson's Labour government prevaricated, the Conservative Party – led by Edward Heath since 1965 – decided to throw caution to the wind.

Having initiated several internal party inquiries, the Leader of the Opposition decided to use his annual speech to the Scottish Conservative Party conference to seize the initiative on devolution. Heath, however, had failed to consult the party adequately, and although his suggestion to appoint the popular former Prime Minister, Sir Alec Douglas-Home, to lead another inquiry into establishing a devolved Scottish Assembly, was bold and imaginative, the general idea went down like a lead balloon with Scottish Tory activists.

Edward Richard George Heath was born in Broadstairs, Kent, and studied at Oxford before war service and election as the MP for Bexley in 1950. He rose quickly through the Tory ranks, serving as Chief Whip and later leading the UK's application to join the European Economic Community. Elected Conservative Party leader in 1965, Heath was Prime Minister between 1970–74.

Still, the speech is significant in that it represented the first time a potential party of government committed itself to devolving power to Scotland, and all the more so given it was the Conservatives. It was, of course, an empty promise, for when Heath did become Prime Minister two years later he forgot all about his 'Declaration of Perth', and the issue of devolution continued to divide his party for another three decades.

SCOTLAND HAS A long history, often gay, sometimes grave, but always characteristically Scottish. You are proud and rightly proud of your traditions... The Conservative Party has always cherished our national traditions. We look to diversity to enrich our national character. The rich variety of our people which has proved to be the glory of our nation.

Yet in the modern fast-moving world – a world of mass industrialisation, mass communication and increasingly complex organisation – there is a constant pressure towards uniformity and centralisation... In the United States power tends to move increasingly away from the States and towards the Federal Government. In Europe countries have combined together in the Common Market and pooled some of their powers in the Central Council of Ministers... [P]eople today demand more efficient services... They demand to see the practice in whatever is the best area of the country applied everywhere. They want to see each problem dealt with by the most specialized group of experts. All this requires Government to become more centralised and to be organised on a larger scale.

Yet, as this happens people suddenly realise that those who take the decisions on these matters – decisions which affect their daily lives in so many different ways – have become more remote. People feel deeply and instinctively that they are taking little part in making or even influencing those decisions...

Scotland has a long history, often gay, sometimes grave, but always characteristically Scottish.

The British have always been proud of their pragmatic approach to these problems. Our lack of a written constitution has given us greater freedom and increased flexibility. In the past we have used this to great advantage to develop our institutions, to meet the changing needs of our society. In this, as in so many other fields, we Conservatives, who have never been doctrinaire, have taken the lead...

And so in this situation I turn again to our basic principles. We find there two important strands. The first is that we have long been the party of Union. We remain the party of Union. Our fundamental belief is in the destiny of the United Kingdom...

The second strand is our belief in the devolution of power. As Quintin Hogg wrote 20 years ago in his book on Conservative philosophy: 'Political liberty is nothing else but the diffusion of power... If power is not to be abused, it must be spread as widely as possible throughout the community'...

It is right that Scotland, which has for so long had her own legal system, her own local authority organisation and her own arrangements in so many other spheres should give a lead in new developments in the way in which she is

Our fundamental belief is in the destiny of the United Kingdom.

governed... Some people want Scotland to remain not only an individual nation but to become a separate country. A country with its own Parliament, its own armed forces, its own customs arrangements, its own seat in the United Nations. This is separatism...

We would propose... the creation of an elected Scottish Assembly, to sit in Scotland. What we have in mind is that this Scottish Assembly would be a single chamber, and would take part in legislation in conjunction with Parliament...

Let there be no doubt about this: the Conservative Party is determined to effect a real improvement in the machinery of government in Scotland. And it is pledged to give the people of Scotland genuine participation in the making of decisions that affect them – all within the historic unity of the United Kingdom.

Nationalism in itself is not an evil, but perverted nationalism, which is really chauvinism, is a menace and danger.

Mick McGahey
1925–1999

SPEECH TO SCOTTISH TRADES UNION CONGRESS • ABERDEEN

18 April 1968

Mick McGahey was one of the giants of the 20th-century trade union movement, and an almost legendary presence within the National Union of Mineworkers. In 1967 he was elected president of the Union's Scottish 'area' and as such articulated the growing mood of militancy among miners following nearly a decade of redundancies and pit closures.

He was also a fine orator, a good example of which can be found below. McGahey's speech to the 1968 Scottish Trades Union Congress in Aberdeen is a real *tour de force*, in which he seeks to reclaim Scottish Nationalism for trade unionism and reconcile it with the fraternal inter-nationalism he had imbibed from his long involvement of the Communist Party of Great Britain.

Michael 'Mick' McGahey was born in Lanarkshire in 1925, the son of a coalminer. He left school at 14 and spent the next quarter of a century working as a miner. McGahey also became active in the NUM and Young Communist League, joining the former's Scottish executive in 1958. He later rose to become the NUM's vice-president and played a prominent role in the miners' strikes of the 1970s and '80s.

It did the trick, and McGahey's motion calling upon 'the Government to introduce legislation to establish a Parliament for Scotland'[31] committed the STUC to devolution six years before the Scottish Council of the Labour Party. His speech (below) was reported in the 71st Annual Report of the Scottish Trades Union Congress.

NATIONALISM IN ITSELF was not an evil, but perverted nationalism, which was really chauvinism, was a menace and danger; he hoped that none would ascribe to the Scottish miners chauvinist motives. Healthy nationalism – love of one's own country, love of one's own people and pride in their traditional militancy and progressiveness – enabled a country to be truly internationalist, and helped it to appreciate all the more the struggles of other nations in their fight for independence.

The Scottish miners believed in the right of national expression in order to
encourage the flowering of all that was good in a country and in a people.
The Scottish miners were proud of their international solidarity and had a record
in this respect that was widely acknowledged. Politically, he himself was a
Communist and the basis of his philosophy was international working class
solidarity; he gave second place to none in his loyalty to the international
working-class movement.

He firmly believed, and his union firmly believed, that Scotland was a nation.
Not a region of Britain, not a district, but a nation in its own right and entitled to
demand to right to nationhood. This was why his union were calling for a

Give the Scottish nation the right to decide their own destiny and their future.

Scottish Parliament; to give the Scottish nation the right to decide their own
destiny and their future.

He knew that there were some people who might infer from this that the
Scottish people believed in setting up a customs barrier and issuing passports.
There might even be some delegates present of this way of thinking, but that was
not his union's concern. What his union were stating was that if Scotland was a
nation, Scotland was entitled to nationhood and the Scottish people were entitled
to decide the form and power of their own institutions. Anything less would be to
deny them nationhood and independence.

The Scottish National Party were not the custodians of true Scottish
nationalism. The best nationalists in Scotland were represented in the Scottish
TUC and in the Scottish Labour Movement. Congress itself had done more in any
12 months for the Scottish people, the Scottish economy, and the Scottish nation
than Mrs Ewing or anyone else in the SNP...

It was said that a Scottish Parliament, with its forms and powers to be
decided by the Scottish electorate, would mean separatism. His colleagues
and he rejected outrightly the theory of separating Scotland from the United
Kingdom, nor did they accept the theory of a classless Scotland at the present
stage. They had more in common with the London dockers, the Durham miners
and the Sheffield engineers than they ever had with the barons and landlord
traitors of that kind in Scotland.

If socialism meant anything at all it meant the decentralisation of power.

The real question at issue was which Scotland delegates supported. Was it
the Scotland of the barons and the landlords, those who had betrayed Scotland
for generations, or the Scotland of the working class? The latter comprised the
true sons and daughters of Scotland, those who by their skills, culture, and

progressive traditions had enriched the Scottish nation. It was these to whom his union referred when they spoke of Scotland and Scotland as a nation.

Was the feasibility of a Scottish Parliament, working within the orbit of a United Kingdom, something far-fetched? Was federalism or the idea of a federation something new? It already existed in what one termed the United States, and it existed in the socialist countries in the Soviet Union, and in Yugoslavia...

He believed in the principles of socialism and was convinced that if socialism meant anything at all it meant decentralisation of power in order to involve the people of a country in the operation of power at every possible level. Development along these lines, in his opinion, would bring to the people of Scotland a Parliament that would enable them to play their part in taking up the challenge of life and contributing to the strength of the international working-class movement.

A rat race is for rats.
We're not rats.

Jimmy Reid
1932–2010

RECTORIAL ADDRESS • UNIVERSITY OF GLASGOW

28 APRIL 1972

The charismatic trade unionist Jimmy Reid was already a household name by the time he addressed students at Glasgow University on accepting his election as Rector in April 1972. The previous year he had led the Upper Clyde Shipbuilders work-in to resist the Conservative government's plan to close the Glasgow shipyards. In a famous speech, Reid implored the workers to show discipline. 'And there will be no hooliganism, there will be no vandalism, there will be no bevvying,' he bellowed, 'because the world is watching us, and it is our responsibility to conduct ourselves with responsibility, and with dignity, and with maturity.'

Jimmy Reid was born in Govan, where he would live and work for much of his life. Initially a Communist, he later joined Labour before migrating to the Scottish National Party after becoming disillusioned with Tony Blair's premiership. Unsuccessful in every election he contested, Reid made more of a mark as a journalist, broadcaster and, of course, as an orator.

Reid's speech at Glasgow University was of a different order, but equally stirring, outlining his then Communist political philosophy and unshakeable faith in human nature, its needs and potential, an analysis which – re-reading it now – seems to anticipate the Thatcherite revolution which at that time was no more than a twinkle in the then Education Secretary's eye.

Much quoted following his death in 2010, Reid's Rectorial address had an immediate impact, and not just in Scotland. *The New York Times* printed it verbatim, generously describing it as 'the greatest speech since President Lincoln's Gettysburg address'.

ALIENATION IS THE PRECISE and correctly applied word for describing the major social problem in Britain today. People feel alienated by society. In some intellectual circles it is treated almost as a new phenomenon. It has, however, been with us for years. What I believe is true is that today it is more widespread, more pervasive than ever before. Let me right at the outset define what I mean by alienation. It is the cry of men who feel themselves the victims of blind economic forces beyond their control.

It's the frustration of ordinary people excluded from the processes of decision-making. The feeling of despair and hopelessness that pervades people who feel with justification that they have no real say in shaping or determining their own destinies.Many may not have rationalised it. May not even understand, may not be able to articulate it. But they feel it. It therefore conditions and colours their social attitudes...

Society and its prevailing sense of values leads to another form of alienation. It alienates some from humanity. It partially de-humanises some people, makes them insensitive, ruthless in their handling of fellow human beings, self-centred and grasping. The irony is, they are often considered normal and well-adjusted. It is my sincere contention that anyone who can be totally adjusted to our society is in greater need of psychiatric analysis and treatment than anyone else...

It is easy and tempting to hate such people. However, it is wrong. They are as much products of society, and of a consequence of that society, human alienation, as the poor drop-out. They are losers. They have lost the essential

*It is the cry of men who feel themselves
the victims of blind economic forces beyond their control.*

elements of our common humanity. Man is a social being. Real fulfilment for any person lies in service to his fellow men and women. The big challenge to our civilisation is not... permissiveness, although I agree our society is too permissive. Any society which, for example, permits over one million people to be unemployed is far too permissive for my liking. Nor is it moral laxity in the narrow sense that this word is generally employed – although in a sense here we come nearer to the problem. It does involve morality, ethics, and our concept of human values. The challenge we face is that of rooting out anything and everything that distorts and devalues human relations...

[One] is the widespread, implicit acceptance of the concept and term 'the rat race'. The picture it conjures up is one where we are scurrying around scrambling for position, trampling on others, back-stabbing, all in pursuit of personal success. Even genuinely intended, friendly advice can sometimes take the form of someone saying to you, 'Listen, you look after number one'. Or as they say in London, 'Bang the bell, Jack, I'm on the bus'.

To the students [of Glasgow University] I address this appeal. Reject these

*Alienation is the precise and correctly applied word
for describing the major social problem in Britain today.*

attitudes. Reject the values and false morality that underlie these attitudes. A rat race is for rats. We're not rats. We're human beings. Reject the insidious pressures in society that would blunt your critical faculties to all that is happening around you, that would caution silence in the face of injustice lest you jeopardise your chances of promotion and self-advancement. This is how it starts, and before you know where you are, you're a fully paid-up member of the rat-pack. The price is too high. It entails the loss of your dignity and human spirit. Or as Christ put it, 'What doth it profit a man if he gain the whole world and suffer the loss of his soul?'

It is the cry of men who feel themselves the victims of blind economic forces beyond their control.

Profit is the sole criterion used by the establishment to evaluate economic activity. From the rat race to lame ducks. The vocabulary in vogue is a give-away. It's more reminiscent of a human menagerie than human society... Government by the people for the people becomes meaningless unless it includes major economic decision-making by the people for the people. This is not simply an economic matter. In essence it is an ethical and moral question, for whoever takes the important economic decisions in society *ipso facto* determines the social priorities of that society.

It is the comprehensive school that is on trial today.

RF Mackenzie
1910–1987

SPEECH PRIOR TO SACKING AS
HEADMASTER OF SUMMERHILL SCHOOL • ABERDEEN

1 APRIL 1974

Even by the time RF Mackenzie was appointed head teacher of Summerhill School by the Labour-controlled Aberdeen Council in 1968, he was a controversial figure. He had for long advocated the abolition of corporal punishment while promoting a 'progressive' curriculum in secondary schools. Furthermore, Mackenzie published his thinking in a series of books in which he challenged the dominance of exams and a utilitarian educational ethos.

Mackenzie's stewardship of Summerhill was not a happy period. Management was not his strong point, and soon there was an orchestrated campaign to remove him. When members of staff descended into two warring factions over plans to phase out use of the belt, Mackenzie's fate was sealed.

This speech, which unfortunately does not seem to have survived in full, took place at a special meeting of Aberdeen Council's Education Committee, convened to decide Mackenzie's future. When he refused to abide by the rules with regard to the use of corporal punishment in his school, a majority vote suspended from duty. He was 64, and would never return to Summerhill. The journalist Harry Reid, who covered the meeting for *The Scotsman*, later recalled that the 'atmosphere was like that of a trial'.

RF Mackenzie was one of the most original and controversial thinkers in 20th century Scotland. Born in Aberdeenshire in 1910, following active service in the RAF during the Second World War, he qualified as a teacher. Mackenzie published several books and died in 1987.

WE'RE JUST AT THE end of an ice age. The ice is beginning to break. When that happens, the thaw comes very quickly. Or again, when the Roman Empire declined, the last bit went down pretty quickly. We're getting near that stage now. There is an urgency about this business that most people don't realise...

I'm glad to have an opportunity of saying publicly that the guilty men are the Scottish Examination Board who go on setting these ridiculous, irrelevant and boring questions...

It is the comprehensive school that is on trial today...

... children with wounds in their souls... We could cure them, we could have cured them, but we were not allowed to, Mr Chairman, because you have given us a divided staff...

They are school pupils, not an army group.

They are nice kids. We want to try to get those with dreadful backgrounds to come with us and not be driven by us... We are moving into new ways of regarding human beings. They are school pupils, not an army group.

The road I intend us to travel may be a bumpy one.

David Steel
1938–

SPEECH TO LIBERAL ASSEMBLY • LLANDUDNO
18 SEPTEMBER 1976

D avid Steel had been Liberal leader for a matter of months at the time he made his first speech to the party's annual Assembly. As Stuart Mole noted in a collection of Steel's speeches, other new leaders would have 'chosen the Assembly to pacify and reassure, to exhort and inspire – and not to throw the Party into controversy or alarm', but 'that was not to be Steel's way'.[32]

Long a supporter of 'realignment' on the political left, as advocated by Steel's patron Jo Grimond, he was determined to nudge his party in this direction after decades of prevaricating. Steel spent the summer handwriting and rewriting his speech at his home in Ettrick Bridge, and although he did not enjoy platform oratory, he had shown throughout his career that he was capable of playing for high stakes.

David Steel was born in 1938, a son of the manse, and part of his childhood was spent in Kenya. He worked for the Scottish Liberal Party before becoming an MP aged only 26. Steel steered the Abortion Act through Parliament in 1967, and was elected Liberal leader in 1976.

Steel's political strategy was already well known, and reports emerged that the Young Liberals were planning a demonstration from the Assembly floor should the word 'coalition' emerge from Steel's lips. But he rejected moves to tone down the text, arguing that if it was not dealt with immediately it would rumble on for years, as under Grimond and Jeremy Thorpe, his immediate predecessor.

Under his guidance, he engineered the Lib/Lab Pact of 1977–78, an Alliance with the SDP in 1981, and finally a merger of the two parties in 1988. In 1999 he became the first Presiding Officer of the Scottish Parliament.

Little did anyone in the hall realise how soon Steel would have an opportunity – via the Lib/Lab Pact – to put his plan into action.

THIS HAS BEEN an extraordinary year for Liberals. We have had three leaders during it, which is some going, even by the standards of Liberal history.

But the particular responsibility of the leader is substantial, and I want to begin by reminding you that I inherit a much stronger Liberal position than did either of my immediate predecessors... In my speech on being elected leader, I declared that there was a generation's work of reform ahead of us. I say that again deliberately. The only trouble is, we haven't got that length of time to do it...

... if we are to succeed as a Party we need certain changes of attitude among others and amongst ourselves. There is no place for the Liberal Party in the soft cosy centre of political debate. We must be away out forward. We must capture the new ground and the high ground of politics...

> There is no place for the Liberal Party
> in the soft cosy centre of political debate.

It is no secret that I count many members of other parties among my friends, that I value their company and discussion with them. But I have long since abandoned hope that their private views may be translated into public action. Even those who occasionally translate private views into public talk are to be found tamely in the lobby when the whip cracks.

The fact that they must face is that if liberal values are to be preserved and developed it can only be through the regeneration of the Liberal Party. Those who have preened themselves as repositories of wisdom and light in the other parties have sold out to the system...

I also said we need to alter attitudes ourselves. I have three things in mind.

First, we've got to be ready and enthusiastic to welcome others into our ranks. I am appalled sometimes by the attitudes of deep suspicion which greets newcomers, particularly if they are nationally known. We must stop behaving like one of the purer sects of the exclusive brethren...

Next, we really must improve our own internal organisation and communication. At the last Party Council meeting, when I spoke of the tortuous nature of our constitution and our procedures and the difficulty of getting quick decisions on anything, I was accused by one of our formidable candidates of seeking to introduce into our Party 'creeping efficiency'. I plead guilty. I don't even ask for galloping efficiency. Creeping efficiency will do.

Third, and most important, we must follow through the logical consequences of our own policies and utterances if we are to convince the public that we really mean business when we talk about being the only agent of hope and change.

Let there be no misunderstanding. We are in being as a political party to form a government so as to introduce the policies for which we stand. That is our clear aim and object. But I as leader have a clear obvious duty to assess how most speedily we can reach that objective. I do not expect to lead just a nice debating society.

> We must stop behaving
> like one of the purer sects of the exclusive brethren.

If we argue that we alone can be the means of transforming the sterility of British political life; if we tell the public that only by voting Liberal in sufficient numbers to prevent one other Party gaining a majority, will we achieve electoral reform, and break the Tory/Labour stranglehold, then equally we must be clear in our own minds that if the political conditions are right (which of course they were not in February, 1974), and if our own values are retained, we shall probably have – at least temporarily – to share power with somebody else to bring about the changes we seek...

Of course neither of the other Parties will want to relinquish their exclusive alternating hold on power, but if the people won't let them have it then they will both have to lump it – Tory and Labour.

I want the Liberal Party to be the fulcrum and centre of the next election argument – not something peripheral to it. If that is to happen we must not give the impression of being afraid to soil our hands with the responsibilities of sharing power.

We must be bold enough to deploy the coalition case positively. We must go all out to attack the other parties for wanting power exclusively to themselves no matter how small a percentage of public support.

> *It is no secret I count many*
> *members of other parties among my friends.*

If people want a more broadly-based government they must vote Liberal to get it. And if they vote Liberal we must be ready to help provide it.

What I am saying is that I want the Liberals to be an altogether tougher and more determined force. I want us to be a crusading and campaigning movement, not an academic think-tank nor minority influence nor occasional safety-valve in the political system.

The road I intend to travel may be a bumpy one, and I recognise therefore the risk that in the course of it we may lose some of the passengers, but I don't mind so long as we arrive at the end of it reasonably intact and ready to achieve our goals.

None of us in this party is interested in office for office's sake. If we were we would never have joined the Liberal Party. But we are fighting to achieve those things in which we believe, for which this party stands, and we must be prepared to do that in the most effective way possible.

It is not beyond the wit of man to devise the institutions to meet those demands and thus strengthen the unity of the United Kingdom.

John P Mackintosh
1929–1978

SPEECH DURING DEBATE ON
SCOTLAND AND WALES BILL • HOUSE OF COMMONS
16 DECEMBER 1976

John P Mackintosh began his career as an academic, penning the standard work on *The British Cabinet* (1962) and, while professor of politics at the University of Strathclyde in the 1960s, *The Devolution of Power: Local Democracy, Regionalism and Nationalism*. When it came to the devolution debates of the late 1960s and '70s, therefore, no one in Parliament emanated more authority on the subject than the Member for Berwick and East Lothian.

John Pitcairn Mackintosh was born in India in 1929, but educated at Melville College and the Universities of Edinburgh and Oxford. He held various lecturing jobs in the 1950s and '60s, and was elected the MP for Berwick and East Lothian in 1966 which, with a six-month interregnum in 1974, Mackintosh held until his death in 1978.

But Mackintosh's genuine commitment to devolution, shared by other Labour MPs at that time such as Donald Dewar, put him out of favour with the party hierarchy, and ministerial office eluded him. A story did the rounds in 1967 that Harold Wilson had commented to his long-serving Secretary of State for Scotland, Willie Ross, 'You had better keep an eye on that man Mackintosh, Willie. He wants your job.' 'No, Harold,' came Ross's reply. 'He wants yours!'

This typically erudite speech came during Parliamentary consideration of the Scotland and Wales Bill, which fell the following year. Tragically, Mackintosh died before its successor, the Scotland Bill, received Royal Assent, although no doubt he would have been dismayed at its rejection in the referendum of March 1979. The final line of this speech is now immortalised in the Scottish Parliament building at Holyrood.

THERE IS A DESIRE for democratic control of the Scottish Administration. There is a recognition of certain national feelings, which are not aggressive. There are cultural and unitary feelings in Scotland, and there is a desire for greater control over the quality of life and other areas of importance in the Scottish environment. This concern is positive and is a valuable addition to the quality of government. I turn to the Bill itself, about which I have some difficulties and reservations. On top of a generally correct approach, it takes all those matters that are the responsibility of the Scottish Administration and devolves them to a Scottish Parliament...

I am unhappy about the powers that are reserved to the Secretary of State. The Secretary of State is a man who will be transformed from the person who actually governs Scotland to the person who will watch over the Assembly while it governs Scotland. The situation may be potentially dangerous when the Secretary of State may be of a different political party from that in the majority at the Assembly. That may cause trouble and difficulty. I should prefer to see much more wholehearted devolution of powers, such as the powers that were laid down in the Government of Ireland Act 1920, which was defended by the right hon. Member for Down, South [Enoch Powell] during its period of existence. That is the kind of clear cut allocation of powers we should have, and I hope that in the passage of the Bill through the House the Lord President of the Council and the Minister of State in the Privy Council Office will allow us to amend the Bill to give more generous powers in areas suitable for Scottish administration...

> I should prefer to see a mush
> more wholehearted devolution of powers.

I see no reason why the royalties on Scottish oil should not be given to the Assembly. They are a fixed amount, and with the addition of personal income tax they would virtually cover the total sum at present covered by the block grant. But it is vital that the money should be devolved in such a way that Treasury control cannot be exerted day by day, month by month and year by year over the Assembly, because that would produce the kind of conflict and subordination which it is the objective of the Bill to prevent...

I want to say a word or two now on the aspect of the electoral system. I hope that my right hon Friend the Lord President [Michael Foot] will consider an amendment advocating a system of proportional representation. I put the case quite simply. For years I taught the value of the British first-past-the-post system in my days as an academic teacher of this subject. It has great merit for a two-party system. If there are two parties and they win 95 per cent of the vote between them, the system has merits. But Scottish politics now has a three-and-a-half or four-party system. Any one of the parties could slip ahead and get 32 per cent of the vote and secure majority in the Assembly. Hon Members have to remember that it is to be a four-year fixed Parliament. It means that a gust of opinion at the appropriate moment giving 32 per cent of the vote could saddle Scotland with a one party majority for the full four years on one-third of the popular vote. That is an unsatisfactory and unstable situation. I was unhappy when the lawyer leading for the Conservative Party opened the debate and said not a word about the Conservative Party's proposals. I was unhappy about that because I suspect that the support for devolution from the Conservative Front Bench is a hoax. I suspect also that this is why the hon Member for Edinburgh, Pentlands [Mr Rifkind] and the hon Member for North Angus and Mearns [Mr Buchanan-Smith] resigned their posts. For years they have said that they did not want this kind of devolution. There was no problem for them in voting against the Bill, because they have never supported this kind of devolution. But there I believe their feeling is that, if the Tories ever won an election, that would be the end of any commitment to devolution among them now. That is very dangerous.

I should prefer to see a mush more wholehearted devolution of powers.

What will happen if that is the case and if the situation in Scotland remains the same is that we shall get a confrontation between Unionism and separatism. We shall get exactly what the right hon Member for Down, South wants or what he thinks is satisfactory – that either the British nation asserts itself or the Scottish nation asserts itself but that they cannot coexist in their national consideration. I reject that proposal. I think that we can be both British and Scottish or British and Welsh. One party, with which I have much sympathy – the nationalists – says 'If you feel Scottish and want to run your own affairs, you must have the full panoply of statehood – with an army, a navy, an air force, ambassadors abroad and the lot'. I do not think that the Scottish people want that. The other group, the Unionists, say 'If you feel British, if you value British traditions and respect British parliamentary democracy, and if you think that the big industries have to cover the whole of Britain, you cannot have a degree of self-government which reflects your needs in your own areas.' I reject both propositions. Institutions have to be the servants of political demands. We have people in Scotland who want a degree of government for themselves at the Scottish level. It is not beyond the wit of man to devise the institutions to meet those demands and thus strengthen the unity of the United Kingdom. I support the measure.

The devolutionary coach...will be on a motorway without exit roads
to a separate Scottish State.

Tam Dalyell
1932–

SPEECH DURING DEBATE ON
THE SCOTLAND BILL • HOUSE OF COMMONS

14 NOVEMBER 1977

On 3 November 1977 Tam Dalyell had already asked, if not actually named, the 'West Lothian Question' (Enoch Powell takes the credit for that), when he pointed out to Prime Minister James Callaghan that under the new Scotland Bill, he would 'still be able to vote on many matters in relation to West Bromwich but not West Lothian'.

Eleven days later Dalyell – whose constituency was then called West Lothian – fleshed out his argument during Commons consideration of the Scotland Bill. Re-reading his speech now, it was – from a Unionist perspective – remarkably prescient. Indeed, Dalyell was one of the most articulate critics of his own government's plans for devolution; he even published a book on the subject entitled *Devolution: The End of Britain?* that same year.

Although the former Lord Chancellor Derry Irvine said the best thing to do about the West Lothian Question was to stop asking it, Dalyell's point persists now devolution is a reality. Along with his long-standing campaign for the truth about the sinking of the *Belgrano* during the Falklands War, it remains the issue with which Dalyell is most closely associated.

Sir Thomas Dalyell Loch of the Binns, 11th Baronet – better known as Tam Dalyell – was born in Edinburgh in 1932 and inherited the Baronetcy of the Binns via his mother in 1972. Educated at the Edinburgh Academy and Eton College, he did his National Service with the Royal Scots Greys before studying history and economics at King's College, Cambridge. Dalyell then became a teacher and entered Parliament following a by-election in 1962. He became Father of the House in 2001 and left the Commons four years later.

ONE OF THE MAJOR objections to the Bill is that it provides not the remotest chance of a lasting settlement between Scotland and England. Do any of us believe, wherever we sit in the House and on whatever side of the devolution argument we have been, that the governmental arrangements formulated in the 1977 Scotland Bill will still be operational in 1987 or 1990?...

The Bill is a stepping stone to further changes of some kind or another. It is not a stable resting place for five or ten years, let alone centuries…

the West Lothian–West Bromwich question problem pinpoints a basic design fault in the steering of the devolutionary coach.

The truth is that the West Lothian–West Bromwich problem is not a minor hitch to be overcome by rearranging the seating in the devolutionary coach. On the contrary, the West Lothian–West Bromwich problem pinpoints a basic design fault in the steering of the devolutionary coach which will cause it to crash into the side of the road before it has gone a hundred miles. For how long will English constituencies and English hon Members tolerate not just 71 Scots, 36 Welsh and a number of Ulstermen but at least 119 hon Members from Scotland, Wales and Northern Ireland exercising an important, and probably often decisive, effect on English politics while they themselves have no say in the same matters in Scotland, Wales and Ireland…

A second of my lengthy list of reasons why this proposed settlement cannot conceivably endure and will have the life of a butterfly lies with the inevitable frustration of the Assemblymen being unable to honour the promises that they have made on account of what they would claim are lack of powers over the economy from Westminster and lack of money from a parsimonious English Treasury that is unwilling to allocate oil revenues. Within weeks of arriving at the High School they will be clamouring for more. Not only will the SNP Members clamour for more, but the Conservative and Labour Members will also do so. Everyone in the Assembly will be united in clamouring for more…

We are voting tonight to jump from the bank of the river on to a log raft which is bound to break up as we are carried downstream to a separate Scottish State. This is a journey upon which this party is united in not wanting to embark. I am sorry that my right hon Friend the Member for Kilmarnock [Mr Ross] is not in the Chamber. When he refers to 'an on-going process – 1926, 1939', some of us must ask 'Where does this on-going process stop?' The logical conclusion is that an 'on-going process' leads to the solution that the SNP want – a separate

We are voting tonight to jump from the bank of the river on to a log raft which is bound to break up.

Scottish State. It is no good saying that we are all involved in an 'on-going process'. If we do not want separation, someone at some time has to make up his mind precisely where this 'on-going process' stops…

I turn now to deal with my vote on the main Question. In the past every one of us has voted for aspects of his or her party's policy about which we were less than enthusiastic. On occasions we have had to swallow and vote. This Bill, however, is different. Public expenditure cuts, Health Service charges and other matters,

On occasion we have had to swallow and vote.

we may dislike. But they are subject to change and alteration. This Bill, if passed, leads to irrevocable consequences. Once an Assembly is established in the High School, I do not see it being abolished in the lifetime of any of us here. We should be saddled with it long after the next election and long after dozens of elections after that – certainly by that time in the form of a separate Scottish Parliament...

Even having said all this, if I thought that the desire for an Assembly in Edinburgh was the considered judgment of the overwhelming majority of the Labour Party members in Scotland I might not have decided to vote against my Government. Indeed, there are many members of the Labour Party in Scotland who, quite honourably, do not think that a Member of Parliament should vote against the three-line Whip. I understand and respect that view. There are a great many fewer who believe nowadays in an Assembly for its own sake...
I confess to irritation with only one group of my hon Friends. It is not the pro-devolvers or those who believe in loyalty to the party come what may. I respect them. My vexation is with those who say 'Of course, when we have got the Assembly we look to folk like you to stop separation.' I reply 'You have no right to say that when you have put such a formidable weapon as an Assembly in the hands of the separatists.' The only difference this time is between those of us who think that we have to take on separatism now and others who judge that we can fend off the challenge later. By that time – this is my judgment – the devolutionary coach, if this Bill is passed, will be on a motorway without exit roads to a separate Scottish State – a journey on which my right hon and hon Friends are unwilling to embark.

There is an episode in the life of Saint Andrew, the patron saint of Scotland, which can serve as an example for what I wish to tell you.

Pope John Paul II
1920–2005

ADDRESS TO THE YOUNG PEOPLE OF SCOTLAND
MURRAYFIELD STADIUM • EDINBURGH
31 MAY 1982

I
n 1982, Pope John Paul II was at the height of what *Spitting Image* liked to portray as his international celebrity. On a pastoral visit to the United Kingdom that May, the Holy Father spent a day and a half of his tour in Scotland. Most famous is the Glasgow leg of that visit, where the Pontiff addressed an open-air Mass in Bellahouston Park.

Blessed Pope John Paul II was born Karol Józef Wojtyła in Wadowice, Poland, in 1920. An athletic child, he attended Krakow's Jagiellonian University in 1938 and thereafter secretly trained as a priest during the Second World War. John Paul became the bishop of Ombi in 1958 and then the archbishop of Krakow six years later. Made a cardinal in 1967, he became the first non-Italian pope in more than four centuries in 1978.

In Edinburgh, however, the focus was on youth, always something close to the Pontiff's heart. Accordingly, he addressed the 'young people of Scotland' at Murrayfield Stadium, more often home to rugby fixtures rather than papal pronouncements. The reception was ecstatic, and indeed video footage of the speech reveals the Pope's apparent irritation at regular interruptions by chanting and cheering. Impressively, he concluded his Murrayfield address with some words of Gaelic.

D
EAR YOUNG PEOPLE of Scotland! Thank you for such warm words of welcome. I am happy that my first contact is with you, the pride of your beloved country and the promise of its bright future! You are at the great crossroads of your lives and you must decide how your future can be lived happily, accepting the responsibilities which you hope will be placed squarely on your shoulders, playing an active role in the world around you. You ask me for encouragement and guidance, and most willingly I offer some words of advice to all of you, in the name of Jesus Christ.

In the first place I say this: you must never think that you are alone in deciding your future! And secondly: when deciding your future, you must not decide for yourself alone! There is an episode in the life of Saint Andrew, the patron saint of Scotland, which can serve as an example for what I wish to tell you. Jesus had been teaching a crowd of five thousand people about the Kingdom of God. They had listened carefully all day, and as evening approached he did not want to send them away hungry, so he told his disciples to give them something to eat. He said this really to test them, because he knew exactly what he was going to do. One of the disciples – it was Saint Andrew – said: 'There is a small boy here with five barley loaves and two fishes; but what is that between so many?' Jesus took the loaves, blessed them, and gave them out to all who were sitting waiting; he then did the same with the fish, giving out as much as was wanted. Later the disciples collected 12 baskets of the fragments that were left over. Now the point I wish to make is this: Saint Andrew gave Jesus all there was available, and Jesus miraculously fed those 5,000 people and still had something left over. It is exactly the same with your lives. Left alone to face the difficult challenges of life today, you feel conscious of your inadequacy and afraid of what the future may hold for you. But what I say to you is this: place your lives in the hands of Jesus. He will

> You must show a conscientious concern
> that the standard of society fit the plan of God.

accept you, and bless you, and he will make such use of your lives as will be beyond your greatest expectations! In other words: surrender yourselves, like so many loaves and fishes, into the all-powerful, sustaining hands of God and you will find yourselves transformed with 'newness of life', with fullness of life. 'Unload your burden on the Lord, and he will support you'.

It is not of primary importance what walk of life naturally attracts you – industry or commerce, science or engineering, medicine or nursing, the priestly or religious life, or the law, or teaching, or some other form of public service – the principle remains always the same: hand the direction of your life over to Jesus and allow him to transform you and obtain the best results, the one he wishes from you. Only Christianity has given a religious meaning to work and recognizes the spiritual value of technological progress. There is no vocation more religious than work! Saint Benedict used to say to his monks that every implement in the monastery must be regarded as a sacred vessel. A Catholic layman or laywoman is someone who takes work seriously. Why? Because, as Saint Paul says, 'I live now not with my own life, but with the life of Christ who lives in me'; 'Life to me is Christ'...

The clearest description of the work of the Holy Spirit has been given by Saint Paul, who said that the Spirit produces 'love, joy, peace, patience, kindness, goodness, trustfulness, gentleness and self-control'. Qualities such as these are ideal in every walk of life and in all circumstances: at home, with your parents and brothers and sisters; at school, with your teachers and friends; in the factory or at the university; with all the people you meet.

Consequently, your lives cannot be lived in isolation, and even in deciding your future you must always keep in mind your responsibility as Christians towards others. There is no place in your lives for apathy or indifference to the world around you. There is no place in the Church for selfishness. You must show a conscientious concern that the standards of society fit the plan of God. Christ counts on you, so that the effects of his Holy Spirit may radiate from you to others and in that way permeate every aspect of the public and the private sector of national life...

You are at the great crossroads of your life.

Follow the example of Our Blessed Lady, the perfect model of trust in God and wholehearted cooperation in his divine plan for the salvation of mankind. Keep in mind the advice she gave the servants at Cana: 'Do whatever he tells you'. Jesus changed the water into wine for his mother on that occasion. Through her intercession he will transform your lives.

I must continue now with my pilgrimage through your beloved Scotland. I take leave of you happy in the thought that your young hearts accompany me on my journey, and that I have the support of your daily prayers. For my part I wish to assure you, each and every one of you, of my love in Christ Jesus. Young people of Scotland, I thank you. Keep the faith joyfully; and my blessing be with you. Oìgridh na h-Alba, tha mi toirt taing dhùibh. Cumaibh an creideamh gu sòlasach; agus mo bheannachd leibh.

It is not the creation of wealth that is wrong but love of money for its own sake.

Margaret Thatcher
1925–

SPEECH TO THE GENERAL ASSEMBLY
OF THE CHURCH OF SCOTLAND • EDINBURGH

21 MAY 1988

Ironically, Margaret Thatcher's controversial speech to the General Assembly of the Church of Scotland in May 1988 was supposed to woo Scots in the wake of a disastrous general election result, in which the Conservative Party lost all but ten of its Scottish MPs. Instead her speech, later dubbed the 'Sermon on the Mound' (a soubriquet Thatcher considered tasteless), created an almost hysterical reaction and quickly became a standard reference point for the Thatcher era in Scotland.

The idea for Thatcher to address the General Assembly, something a premier can do only by invitation, actually came from Malcolm Rifkind, Secretary of State for Scotland since 1986. 'I do not generally hold with politicians preaching sermons,' Thatcher wrote in the second volume of her memoirs, *The Path to Power*,[33] 'though since so many clerics preach politics there seems no room in this regard for restrictive practices.' Raised a Methodist, Thatcher was genuinely interested in theology and intended to give the Kirk a very personal interpretation of the gospel.

Margaret Thatcher was born in 1925 in Grantham, a small market town in eastern England, and she later rose to become the first (and for two decades the only) woman to lead a major Western democracy. Thatcher won three successive general elections and served as UK Prime Minister for more than 11 years (1979–90), a record unmatched in the 20th century.

As a result, the so-called Sermon on the Mound was probably one of most thoroughly prepared speeches Mrs Thatcher ever delivered. The mythmakers, however, went to town, so much so that historians subsequently described the speech being greeted by 'stony silence' rather than the warm applause it actually received. Others were kinder. 'As a public speaker… she was robust, challenging, clear, and a scourge of soft thinking and complacency,' wrote Harry Reid in his bestselling book on the Church of Scotland, *Outside Verdict*,[34] 'and these are among the qualities that I for one would look for in a great preacher.'

M AY I... SAY A few words about my personal belief in the relevance of
Christianity to public policy – to the things that are Caesar's?

The Old Testament lays down in Exodus the Ten Commandments as given
to Moses, the injunction in Leviticus to love our neighbour as ourselves and
generally the importance of observing a strict code of law. The New Testament is
a record of the Incarnation, the teachings of Christ and the establishment of the
Kingdom of God. Again we have the emphasis on loving our neighbour as
ourselves and to 'Do-as-you-would-be-done-by'.

I believe that by taking together these key elements from the Old and New
Testaments, we gain: a view of the universe, a proper attitude to work, and
principles to shape economic and social life.

We can't blame society if we disobey the law.

We are told we must work and use our talents to create wealth. 'If a man will
not work he shall not eat' wrote St Paul to the Thessalonians. Indeed, abundance
rather than poverty has a legitimacy which derives from the very nature of
Creation.

Nevertheless, the Tenth Commandment – Thou shalt not covet – recognises
that making money and owning things could become selfish activities. But it is
not the creation of wealth that is wrong but love of money for its own sake.
The spiritual dimension comes in deciding what one does with the wealth.
How could we respond to the many calls for help, or invest for the future, or
support the wonderful artists and craftsmen whose work also glorifies God,
unless we had first worked hard and used our talents to create the necessary
wealth? And remember the woman with the alabaster jar of ointment...

None of this, of course, tells us exactly what kind of political and social
institutions we should have. On this point, Christians will very often genuinely
disagree, though it is a mark of Christian manners that they will do so with
courtesy and mutual respect. (Applause.) What is certain, however, is that any set
of social and economic arrangements which is not founded on the acceptance of
individual responsibility will do nothing but harm.

We are all responsible for our own actions. We can't blame society if we
disobey the law. We simply can't delegate the exercise of mercy and generosity to

Intervention by the state must never become so great it effectively removes personal responsibility.

others. The politicians and other secular powers should strive by their measures
to bring out the good in people and to fight down the bad: but they can't create
the one or abolish the other. They can only see that the laws encourage the best
instincts and convictions of the people, instincts and convictions which I'm
convinced are far more deeply rooted than is often supposed...

We must recognise that modern society is infinitely more complex than that of Biblical times and of course new occasions teach new duties. In our generation, the only way we can ensure that no one is left without sustenance, help or opportunity, is to have laws to provide for health and education, pensions for the elderly, succour for the sick and disabled.

But intervention by the State must never become so great that it effectively removes personal responsibility. The same applies to taxation; for while you and I would work extremely hard whatever the circumstances, there are undoubtedly some who would not unless the incentive was there. And we need their efforts too...

Nevertheless I am an enthusiast for democracy. And I take that position, not because I believe majority opinion is inevitably right or true – indeed no majority can take away God-given human rights – but because I believe it most effectively safeguards the value of the individual, and, more than any other system, restrains the abuse of power by the few. And that is a Christian concept.

But there is little hope for democracy if the hearts of men and women in democratic societies cannot be touched by a call to something greater than themselves. Political structures, state institutions, collective ideals – these are not enough.

We Parliamentarians can legislate for the rule of law. You, the Church, can teach the life of faith...

Margaret Thatcher: complete public statements 1945–1990. Database and Compilation © OUP 1999.

Well, we say yes and we are the people.

Canon Kenyon Wright
1932–

SPEECH AT INAUGURAL MEETING OF THE
SCOTTISH CONSTITUTIONAL CONVENTION • EDINBURGH

30 MARCH 1989

An Episcopalian clergyman was an unlikely standard bearer for devolution, but then during the 1980s and '90s lots of unusual things happened in Scottish politics. The son of a textile technician, Canon Kenyon Wright had become, in 1981, General Secretary of the Scottish Council of Churches, the berth from which he became an influential figure in the campaign for a Scottish Parliament.

Talk of a cross-party 'constitutional convention' had been in the air since the early 1980s, but only in 1988 when the Claim of Right was signed (calling for a devolved Parliament) did it get off the ground. Initially, it looked as though every opposition party in Scotland would agree to take part in the Convention – the primary aim of which was to draw up a blueprint for devolution – but when the SNP (which had signed the Claim of Right) withdrew in early 1989, the exercise proceeded with just Labour, the Liberal Democrats and representatives from what became known as 'civic Scotland'.

Canon Kenyon Wright was born in Paisley and worked as a missionary in India before returning to the UK to take up various Anglican and ecumenical appointments. After chairing the Scottish Constitutional Convention he was a prominent campaigner in the 1997 devolution referendum, and stood for the Scottish Parliament twice, having joined the Liberal Democrats in 2000.

On 30 March 1989 the Scottish Constitutional Convention met for the first time in the hall usually reserved for meetings of the General Assembly of the Church of Scotland. Kenyon Wright was appointed executive chairman and made a memorable opening speech. Later he wrote that as he was preparing this, Thatcher had been widely reported as saying 'we are a grandmother' on the birth of a grandchild. 'Playing on that apparent delusion of grandeur', Wright incorporated what the journalist Iain Macwhirter later called 'a marvellously crafted soundbite'.

THIS IS A MOMENT for quiet thankfulness and for firm resolution – and, yes, for at least a measure of solemn joy. You are making history here today. You are witnessing a minor miracle. Not in living memory, indeed not for very much longer than that, has there been a gathering in Scotland remotely comparable to this.

We begin therefore not with an apology nor with a political argument but with a confident assertion. We represent Scotland. There is no false exaggeration in that claim.

The Scottish Constitutional Convention which meets today for the first time in this hall includes more than 80 per cent of Scotland's MPs, includes representatives of every single regional and island council throughout our land and of the overwhelming majority of district authorities. From the great cities of Glasgow, Edinburgh, Aberdeen and Dundee to the remotest Highland communities, from the ancient burghs of Scotland, from the Borders to the Western and Northern Isles, the representatives of the people are here.

At the risk of offending some of my political friends, I dare to say that by any standard of measurement we are much more representative collectively of Scotland than the Westminster parliament is of the United Kingdom.

> *We represent Scotland.*
> *There is no false exaggeration in that claim.*

But when, as I hope we will do today, we pass together the declaration which I now present to you, then we will represent Scotland in an even deeper and more important sense. We are not met here to make claims for ourselves. We are met to make a claim for Scotland, and to set our hands to the task of giving substance to that claim. The declaration is first a constitutional Claim of Right and then second a costly commitment of the consequences of that claim.

Our Claim of Right is firmly based on our nation's past – but it is not about the past, it is very much about what is happening to us now and the need to save our nation from a constitutional crisis, and from a deadly assault, on our identity and our deeply held values. This is not just a constitutional claim, it is a moral claim. It is not only about past history but about present justice. It is not just about politics but about people...

It is our purpose to look beyond the symptoms to the constitutional disease. Again and again and again on something like 33 different occasions in the life of this parliament, it has debated measures which affected quite fundamentally Scotland's national institutions and the quality of life of our people. Again and again and again the elected representatives of the Scottish people have voted by [a] margin of 6 to 1 against these damaging policies. Again and again and again parliament has imposed these on Scotland.

Our claim then is clear and unmistakable but we are not ourselves a Scottish parliament or assembly. We are a constitutional convention, authorised not by Westminster but by the historic Scottish understanding of constitutional power, and by the people. We have a limited and definite task and the second part of the declaration spells out in three simple sentences what that task is...

Our first commitment is 'to agree a scheme for an assembly or parliament for Scotland'. Can we do that? It will certainly be no easy task but two things are clear. First, any scheme we put forward must be consensus, the highest common factor of our common thinking, which gives to no political grouping or party everything it wants but which the Scottish people whatever their many differing views can see as a real and viable proposal for at least the next step. Second, we have a lot of hard work before us for any such scheme must not just be a general idea, it must be carefully worked out in detail.

It is not only about past history but about present justice.

This brings us to the second remit, 'to mobilise Scottish opinion and secure the approval of the Scottish people for that scheme'. We have been pressed to say how that approval will be sought. Our answer must be that that is an open question which must be decided in the light of the actual circumstances when a scheme is produced. More important, there must be over the next year a massive and constant process of debate, discussion and questioning all over Scotland...

But what of implementation? The question is already being asked in some quarters, 'If we produce a detailed scheme which has the backing of Scotland's people, what happens if that other voice we all know so well responds by saying, 'We say no and we are the state?' Well, we say yes and we are the people and in the last analysis, Scotland believes not in the 'Royal we' but in 'we the people'. I have no detailed answer to my question but I know this: our task could not be more important and if we succeed in producing a scheme and in ensuring that the people of Scotland own that as fully and as comprehensively as possible, there will be no turning back. We will find a way.

I hate being Scottish.
We're the lowest of the fucking low.

Renton

FICTIONAL

SPEECH IN THE MIDDLE OF A MOOR • SOMEWHERE IN SCOTLAND

1990S

In the 1996 film *Trainspotting*, based on the 1993 novel by Irvine Welsh, the viewer watches as the characters Renton, Spud, Tommy and Sick Boy (all heroin addicts whom the movie follows in an economically deprived part of Edinburgh in the late 1980s) alight from a train in, one assumes, the Scottish Highlands. As the train pulls away they look around, apparently uncertain of what to do next. After some desultory chat, they step across the tracks towards the vast moorland, although everyone but Tommy is visibly bored and unwilling to enjoy the great outdoors. 'Doesn't it make you proud to be Scottish?' asks Tommy, prompting the following peroration from Renton:

Irvine Welsh was born in Leith in 1958. His writing is renowned for its raw Scottish dialect and an equally raw depiction of Edinburgh's underworld. The title of his novel Trainspotting was used as a synonym for 'wasting time'. John Hodge later adapted it into an Academy Award-nominated screenplay.

I HATE BEING SCOTTISH. We're the lowest of the fucking low, the scum of the earth, the most wretched, servile, miserable, pathetic trash that was ever shat into civilization. Some people hate the English, but I don't. They're just wankers. We, on the other hand, are colonized by wankers. We can't even pick a decent culture to be colonized by. We are ruled by effete arseholes. It's a shite state of affairs and all the fresh air in the world will not make any fucking difference.[35]

Instead of going 'back to basics', the Government should be going back to the drawing board.

John Smith
1938–1994

REPLY TO THE QUEEN'S SPEECH • HOUSE OF COMMONS
18 NOVEMBER 1993

In July 1992 John Smith won the Labour leadership convincingly, securing 90.9 per cent of the vote in a complicated electoral college. But he was only leader for 22 months, and his rather cautious approach to opposition provoked some criticism. Two bright young things called Tony Blair and Gordon Brown, for example, reckoned he was complacent in his belief that all it would take to win power at the next general election was 'one more heave'.

John Smith was born in 1938. After graduating from Glasgow University he worked as a lawyer before entering Parliament in 1970. He was the Secretary of State for Trade from 1978–79, and then Shadow Chancellor of the Exchequer under Neil Kinnock from 1987–92.

But Smith was a moderniser in certain important respects, fighting hard to introduce the principle of one-member, one-vote for the selection of Labour candidates. On policy issues, he moved more slowly, although the increasing unpopularity of John Major's scandal-hit government increased popular support for his party. And no one doubted Smith's ability to take advantage of that growing unpopularity.

Brian Brivati reckoned Smith's reply to the 1993 Queen's Speech was 'one of his finest House of Commons performances. It combined the sharp jabbing of political attack with some reasoned alternatives to the current plans laid out in the Queen's Speech… and it is the obvious preparation and planning coupled with the speed of thought on his feet that comes over in this speech.'[36] The tragedy, of course, is that Smith did not live to see Labour's landslide election victory in 1997.

AT THE CONSERVATIVE party conference the Prime Minister launched his big idea – 'back to basics'. It is true that those magic words do not appear in the Gracious Speech itself. We should perhaps be grateful that Her Majesty was not obliged to repeat the mantra, but there is no doubt that that is the right hon Gentleman's chosen course. He could not have been clearer about it at Blackpool. The Conservative party, he told us, is now going back to basics.

Ever since then political commentators, some bewildered members of the Cabinet and millions of incredulous electors have been trying to work out what the Prime Minister means. The first thought that occurs to them, perhaps not surprisingly, is that the Conservatives have been in government for 14 years. If now we have to go back to basics, what on earth has been happening over 14 years of Conservative Government? Or is this perhaps another coded attack on the glorious achievements of the former Tory leader – another oblique reference to 'the golden age that never was', to quote the Prime Minister's own revealing description of his predecessor's achievements? I hope that there are still some loyal souls on the Tory Benches who will be prepared, as a matter of honour, to rebut such a surreptitious attack on the Thatcher Downing Street years.

We know, of course, that the Prime Minister is haunted by those years and even more troubled by the recent flood of memoirs from former Cabinet Ministers all bearing the same title, *How I almost stood up to Mrs Thatcher*. Her memoirs rather stole the show at the Conservative party conference. Even the Prime Minister's speech could not avoid them. At the start of his speech to the

Surely it is wrong to break election promises as cavalierly as the Government have done.

conference he said: '"Memoirs to the left of me", "Memoirs to the right of me", "Memoirs in front of me", "Volley'd and thundered."' He borrowed the quote from Tennyson's great poem, 'The Charge of the Light Brigade'. Perhaps he should have read on. The poem continues: 'Boldly they rode and well,' 'Into the jaws of Death... ' 'Rode the six hundred.'

I know why the Prime Minister did not finish the quote – there are only 332 Tory Members facing obliteration at the next election. We all know that, after 14 years of Conservative Government, 'back to basics' is no more and no less than an appalling admission of failure. The Conservative party and the Prime Minister have clearly reached the conclusion that they can no longer plausibly defend their record in office, so they are seeking to wipe from our consciousness the fact that they have been in power for the longest single period of any Government since the Second World War and that they – and they alone – after all these years, are responsible for the state of Britain today...

We have been told that part of the intention of the 'back to basics' policy is to teach people the difference between right and wrong and the importance of the acceptance of responsibility. The problem for the Government in that approach is their credibility as teachers and the example of responsibility that they have set. Surely it is wrong to break election promises as cavalierly as the Government have done. Surely it is wrong to impose a tax on the heating of every household in Britain when such an action was expressly excluded before the 1992 election. Surely it is wrong to scapegoat single parents and to stigmatise their children. Surely it is wrong never to resign voluntarily if major errors are made. Surely it is wrong to deny responsibility for policies which have led to mass unemployment and misery for millions of families. Surely it is wrong to have deliberately widened the gap between the rich and poor in our society.

Those are actions of a Government who purport to lecture others about getting 'back to basics'. I believe that 'back to basics' is easily exposed as a political sham, but there are basic needs and aspirations among our people. They want jobs for themselves and for their children. They want a truly national health service which is available to all and which provides the best possible health care proudly in line with the principles of the service's founders. They want well-equipped schools and well-trained and valued teachers to provide opportunities for their children to learn and to succeed. They want decent and affordable homes for their families. They want our industry to compete with the best and to win, for they know that that is the best security for their prosperity.

I regret that the Gracious Speech is irrelevant to the real aspirations and needs of our people. It is so removed from those aspirations that, instead of going 'back to basics', the Government should be going back to the drawing board.

*When someone dies young, as these did,
we tend to think of what they might have been,
of what they were becoming.*

Very Rev Dr James Whyte
1920–2005

SERMON AT MEMORIAL SERVICE FOR VICTIMS
OF THE DUNBLANE MASSACRE • DUNBLANE CATHEDRAL

9 OCTOBER 1996

On 13 March 1996 an unemployed former shopkeeper and Scout leader called Thomas Hamilton walked into the Dunblane Primary School armed with two pistols and two revolvers. He made his way to the school's gymnasium and opened fire on a Primary One class of five- and six-year-old children, killing or wounding all but one. Fifteen pupils died together with their teacher, Gwen Mayor, who naturally tried to protect the children in her care.

Hamilton then left the gymnasium through an emergency exit. He continued shooting outside before returning to the gym and turning one of the guns on himself, dying instantly. The massacre stunned Scotland and the world and when, some months later, a memorial service was arranged at Dunblane Cathedral, the families of the victims requested that the Very Rev Dr James Whyte lead the service.

James Aitken Whyte was born in 1920 and studied philosophy and divinity at Edinburgh University. After his ordination in 1945 he became an army chaplain and parish minister before becoming an academic at St Mary's College, the divinity faculty of the University of St Andrews. Whyte was Moderator of the 1988 General Assembly of the Church of Scotland and died in 2005.

Although it was an unwelcome responsibility, Whyte, as the then moderator of the General Assembly of the Church of Scotland, had put into words the nation's grief following the Lockerbie bombing and, almost eight years later, did so again in different, but equally tragic, circumstances. His sermon, reproduced here, was widely praised.

WHEN THIS MEMORIAL SERVICE was being planned a theme emerged: the theme 'Out of darkness into light'. About the darkness no one had any doubt. Darkness fell on many families and indeed on this entire community on the morning of 13 March. Light was turned into darkness. Yet in a Memorial Service, even after only six months – and six months is a short time in the history of grief – darkness cannot be allowed the last word. 'The light shines in the darkness, and the darkness has not overcome it,' says St John. The last word must still be with light...

Our act of Remembrance today used the symbolism of light. It seems so natural and appropriate. By lighting the candles and by reading the names you, as a community, have remembered before God each individual who died in the massacre on 13 March.

Darkness cannot be allowed the last word.

Each of these candles represents a unique human life.

The candle is a good symbol, especially for the children. It is small, yet it is a bright, warm light. My wife used to teach Primary One, and she wouldn't have exchanged that for any other job in the world, because of her delight in these children, their openness, their eagerness to learn and the brightness they brought into the classroom. So would it be, I'm sure, with Gwen. The Primary One teacher is like a mum to her children.

But the candle is also a symbol of fragility, vulnerability. Is it easily snuffed out. Such is our life, and the life of the child.

Each candle today is a life that we remember, a light that God gave to us, even if for only a little while. When someone dies young, as these did, we tend to think of what they might have been, of what they were becoming. A young woman with so much of her life still before her. Young children at a most delightful stage of their development...

'I am the light of the world,' said Jesus. 'Whoever follows me will not walk in darkness, but will have the light of life.' The text, like our theme, 'out of darkness into light', implies that we all must make a journey. Those who lost a dear one, clearly. The survivors, who lost their innocence that dreadful morning, whose lives are scarred, have their journey to make. And all of us who share the horror, must make our journey out of that horror into a safer, more civilised society...

So we dare not get stuck. When things like this happen, you find yourself cast in a new role – bereaved parent, bereaved family, whatever. It is unbearably painful, but it also confers on you a certain kind of distinction, importance, a new identity. You are a victim. Now that is true. That is the dreadful experience you must come to terms with. But for your children's and the other children's

Each of these candles represents a unique human life.

sakes, you cannot let what happened to you become your whole identity. We must never give the other children the impression that to be valued, a child must be dead. That is to close the door against life, against the future. You are never just a victim. You are who you are, and what you do. The door must open to beckon you, not to forget, never to forget, but to take your experience into the future, though it is a different future from the one you yourself had planned.

I don't think any of us will ever have a completely satisfying explanation of why such terrible things happen in this world, why they happen to us, why they happen to innocent children. Christianity does not offer us an intellectual explanation. It offers us the story of a man on a cross, God's own son sharing our suffering, sharing our darkness, until in him we find the light. He is the victim who became the victor, and gives us the victory too.

Out of darkness into light. 'Whoever follows me,' said Jesus, 'will not walk in darkness, but will have the light of life.'

I said we must each find our own way, our own route, out of darkness into light. Perhaps I should rather have said, 'God has his own way with each of us.' Our ways will be different, but they will, I suspect, have this in common. As we follow him who is the world's true light, we begin to see bits of the jangled, jagged nonsense of our lives falling into place, making some kind of pattern. No loss is a dead loss. In all loss there is gain. The mistakes we have made, the suffering we so regret having caused to others, become occasions to learn and to know more deeply God's forgiveness and his grace. The awful things that have happened, to us, to our children or our friends, may become occasions to know more deeply the infinite value of human love, the strength of human sympathy, and to know, perhaps for the first time, the mystery of the divine love and the serenity that finally banishes resentment and bitterness, and leads us into peace.

May the light of the world go with each of us in our journeyings through life. For he has promised, 'Whoever follows me will not walk in darkness, but will have the light of life.'

Very few ever get a chance in rugby terms to go for Everest, for the top of Everest. You have the chance today.

Jim Telfer
1940–

PRE-MATCH PEP TALK • CAPE TOWN • SOUTH AFRICA

21 JUNE 1997

This speech by assistant coach Jim Telfer – quoted in rugby circles to this day – is from the morning of the British and Irish Lions Test match against the then world champions South Africa. The Lions played three Test matches in the series (ultimately winning the series 2–1) and the 'Everest' speech came just before the first Test.

James 'Jim' Telfer has been a fixture of Scottish rugby since the early 1960s. Born the son of a Borders shepherd in 1940, he went on to captain Scotland and coach his native team as well as the British and Irish Lions. In the 1990s Telfer took over as the Scottish Rugby Union's first full-time director. A third Grand Slam and a Five Nations win bookended that decade and he retired from the game at the end of 2003.

The feeling at the time, certainly in South Africa, was that the brute force of the South African pack of forwards would completely obliterate the Lions' and so Telfer – who was coaching the Lions forwards – felt he needed to galvanise his players in the hours before the game. Huddled together in a mini-scrum, many of the players were visibly moved (judging by the DVD *Living with Lions*), and some even fought back tears.

Playing against South Africa *in* South Africa was generally considered to be the most attritional thing an international rugby player could do. As a South African sports magazine put it at the time, the Lions were a 'nice bunch of blokes who were making a bit of history and, in so doing, winning friends rather than matches'. The Lions, of course, won this match 25–16.

THE EASY BIT has passed. Selection for the Test team is the easy bit. You have an awesome responsibility on the eight individual forwards' shoulders, awesome responsibility. This is your fucking Everest, boys. Very few ever get a chance in rugby terms to go for Everest, for the top of Everest. You have the chance today.

Being picked is the easy bit. To win for the Lions in a Test match is the ultimate, but you'll not do it unless you put your bodies on the line. Every one jack of you for 80 minutes. Defeat doesn't worry me. I've had it often and so have you, it's performance that matters. If you put in the performance, you'll get what you deserve. No luck attached to it. If you don't put it in, then [if] we're honest, then we're second-raters.

They don't rate us, they don't respect us. They don't respect you. They don't rate you. The only way to be rated is to stick one on them, to get us right up in their faces and turn them back, knock them back. Outdo what they can do. Out jump them, out scrum them, out ruck them, out drive them, out tackle them, until they're fucking sick of you.

Defeat doesn't worry me, I've had it often and so have you.

Remember the pledges you made. Remember how you depend on each other, you depend on each other at every phase, teams within teams, scrums, lineouts, ruck ball, tackles.

They are better than you've played against so far. They are better individually or they wouldn't be there. So it's an awesome task you have, it will only be done as I say if everybody commits themself now...

You are privileged. You are the chosen few. Many are considered but few are chosen. They don't think fuck all of us. Nothing. We're here just to make up the fucking numbers... Their weakness is the scrum. Nobody's going to do it for you. You have to find your own solace, your own drive, your own ambition, your own inner strength, because the moment's arrived for the greatest game of your fucking lives.

But today there is a new voice in the land, the voice of a democratic parliament.

Donald Dewar
1937–2000

SPEECH AT OPENING OF THE SCOTTISH PARLIAMENT • EDINBURGH

1 JULY 1999

Since his election to the Westminster Parliament in the 1960s, Donald Dewar had argued consistently for devolution to Scotland, so it was fitting that, when the first elections to the new Scottish Parliament were held in May 1999, he should emerge as its first First Minister. Labour, however, did not have an overall majority – the Parliament's electoral system was designed to make that almost impossible – so a coalition deal was reached with the Liberal Democrats.

Donald Campbell Dewar was born in Glasgow and studied at the city's university before practicing as a solicitor. He entered Parliament in 1966 as the MP for Aberdeen South but lost his seat four years later. He did not rejoin the House of Commons until 1978, when he won the Glasgow Garscadden by-election. Dewar became Secretary of State for Scotland in 1997 and died, in office as First Minister, in 2000.

Once the negotiations were completed, preparations got under way for the official opening of the Scottish Parliament, then sitting in a temporary home on the Mound, at which Her Majesty Queen Elizabeth II was to be present. At first she spoke, then Dewar replied to the Queen's address with a speech thanking her for the Mace, the Parliament's symbol of authority.

The 1 July was a gorgeous summer's day in Edinburgh, and I remember listening to this speech (on a radio) while standing on the Mound. Others watched it on large screens specially erected in Princes Street Gardens. It was a fine speech, and captured the zeitgeist perfectly.

YOUR MAJESTY, on behalf of the people of Scotland I thank you for the gift of the Mace. It is a symbol of the great democratic traditions from which we draw our inspiration and our strength. At its head are inscribed the opening words of our founding statute: 'There shall be a Scottish Parliament'. Through long years, many long years in the case of many of us, those words were first a hope, then a belief, then a promise. Now they are a reality.

This is indeed a moment anchored in our history. Today we can reach back to the long haul to win this parliament, to the struggles of those who brought democracy to Scotland, to that other parliament dissolved in controversy over 300 years ago.

Today we can look forward to the time when this moment will be seen as a turning point – the day when democracy was renewed in Scotland when we revitalised our place in this, our United Kingdom.

This is about more than our politics and our laws. This is about who we are, how we carry ourselves. Distant echoes. And in the quiet moments of today – if there are any – we might hear some echoes from the past: the shout of the welder in the din of the great Clyde shipyards, the speak of the Mearns rooted in the land, the discourse of the Enlightenment when Edinburgh and Glasgow were indeed a light held to the intellectual life of Europe, the wild cry of the great pipes and back to the distant noise of battles in the days of Bruce and Wallace.

The past is part of us, part of every one of us and we respect it. But today there is a new voice in the land, the voice of a democratic parliament, a voice to shape Scotland, a voice above all for the future.

A voice to shape Scotland, a voice above all for the future.

Walter Scott wrote that only a man with soul so dead could have no sense, no feel for his native land. For me – and I think in this I speak at least for any Scot today – this is a proud moment, a new stage in a journey begun long ago and which has no end. This is a proud day for all of us.

A Scottish Parliament, not an end but a means to greater ends and these too are part of our Mace. Woven into the symbolic thistles are these four words – wisdom, justice, compassion, integrity.

Burns would have understood that. We've just heard beautifully sung one of his most enduring works, and at the heart of that song is a very Scottish conviction that honesty and simple dignity are priceless virtues not imparted by rank or birth or privilege but part of the soul.

Burns believed that sense of worth ultimately prevail, he believed that was the core of politics and that without it our profession is inevitably impoverished.

Timeless values: wisdom, justice, compassion, integrity – timeless values, honourable aspirations for this new forum of democracy born on the cusp of a new century.

We are fallible – we all know that. We will make mistakes but I hope and I believe we will never lose sight of what brought us here – the striving to do right by the people of Scotland, to respect their priorities, to better their lot and to contribute to the common weal.

This is about who we are, how we carry ourselves.

I look forward to the days ahead and I know there will be many of them. This chamber will sound with debate, argument and passion, when men and women from all over Scotland will meet to work together for a future built on the first principles of social justice.

But today we pause and reflect. It is a rare privilege in an old nation to open a new parliament. Today is and must be a celebration of the principles, the traditions, the democratic imperatives which have brought us to this point and which will sustain us in the future.

Your Majesty, we are proud that you are here today to hansel this parliament and here with us as we dedicate ourselves to the work that lies ahead. Your Majesty, our thanks.

It is neither in keeping with the spirit of the times nor consistent with the social inclusion that we wish to celebrate in the year of the millennium.

Lord James Douglas-Hamilton
1942–

SPEECH ON THE ACT OF SETTLEMENT · SCOTTISH PARLIAMENT

16 DECEMBER 1999

As a Member of the Scottish Parliament, and indeed as an MP before that, Lord James Douglas-Hamilton was not known as a talented orator, but rather a diligent and clubbable minister at the old Scottish Office. But on occasion, and if the subject was of interest, he could rise to the occasion and deliver a speech that was both heartfelt and lucid.

James Alexander Douglas-Hamilton, Lord Selkirk of Douglas was born in 1942, a younger son of the 14th Duke of Hamilton and Brandon. After Eton, Balliol College, Oxford, and Edinburgh University, he worked as an advocate before being elected the MP for Edinburgh West in 1974. 'Lord James', as he was known, joined the Scottish Office in 1987 and spent an unprecedented ten years as a minister. In 1994 he renounced his peerage in order to avoid a by-election, but was elevated to the House of Lords as a life peer after losing his seat in 1997. From 1999 until 2007 Lord James was a Lothians MSP.

Such an occasion arose when MSPs debated Mike Russell's motion urging that the centuries-old Act of Settlement be repealed. This was originally an act of the old Parliament of England in 1701, which settled the succession to the English throne to the Electress Sophia of Hanover (a grand-daughter of James I) and her Protestant heirs. This act was later extended to Scotland via Article II of the Treaty of Union, enacted in the Acts of Union 1707.

That it barred Roman Catholics from becoming monarch was, and remains, controversial, and in his speech Lord James cited support from a broad range of Scotland's civic, religious and political organisations. The Act remains in force, not least because unpicking it would be a legislative nightmare: given that the current Queen is head of state in several realms, laws governing the succession could only be altered with the consent of all the other realms, as it touches on the succession to the shared throne.

OVER THE PAST 300 YEARS, nothing has precluded any party – including the Labour party, when it was in government – from addressing this issue. I do not recollect its coming before me during the ten years I was in the Government. It has arisen this year as a result of wholesale constitutional reform and the approaching millennium.

The important issue is whether there should be legislation that blatantly discriminates against a Christian religion. The subject is particularly relevant as we live in a multifaith community. In the context of the millennium, it is intended to recognise and appreciate the contribution of all faiths and communities in our

> There are some
> 800,000 Scots of Roman Catholic origin,
> and they deserve better than to have an
> outdated legislation... in force discriminating against them.

country. The heir to the throne can accede if he marries a Muslim, a Buddhist, a scientologist, a Moonie, an atheist or a sun-worshipper, but not if he marries a Roman Catholic. Leaving such a stigma in place when no other religion or faith is singled out is grossly unfair...

The basic truth that was applicable in 1829 and remains so today is that a substantial proportion of our countrymen and countrywomen are of Roman Catholic origin. There are some 800,000 Scots of Roman Catholic origin, and they deserve better than to have outdated legislation, some 300 years old, in force discriminating against them. Only a few years ago, in 1974, there had to be legislation to confirm that a Roman Catholic could be Lord Chancellor.

The Act of Settlement and its corresponding Scottish provisions are, as the First Minister has described them, a 'legacy from the past'. However, as well as being a very unwelcome legacy from the past, it constitutes what Michael Forsyth

> The important issue is whether there should be legislation
> that blatantly discriminates against a Christian religion.

called the British constitution's 'grubby little secret'. The Equal Opportunities Committee of this Parliament calls it an 'anachronistic anomaly', and the cardinal has described it as an 'insult to all Catholics'. It is neither in keeping with the spirit of the times nor consistent with the social inclusion that we wish to celebrate in the year of the millennium.

Our vote today should serve as a signal that blatant and hurtful legislation discriminating against a Christian religion is not acceptable, just as discrimination against a race or ethnic community is not acceptable. Today we have the opportunity to give an example to Britain, by recommending that such discrimination is an offensive anachronism that should be swept away. I commend the motion to the Parliament.

For 300 years, those with power have had access to legal terror.

Tommy Sheridan
1964–

SPEECH DURING DEBATE ON ABOLITION
OF POINDINGS AND WARRANT SALES BILL · SCOTTISH PARLIAMENT

27 APRIL 2000

For anyone who covered the early years of the Scottish Parliament, Tommy Sheridan, the Glasgow MSP and leader of the Scottish Socialist Party, was a charismatic presence. At that time his party's only Parliamentary representative, it fell to Sheridan to convince Scottish political opinion that socialism was not an anachronism.

Tommy Sheridan was born in Pollok in 1964 and educated at Lourdes Secondary in Glasgow. After Stirling University he campaigned against the Community Charge in Scotland and became President of the Anti-Poll Tax Federation. In 1992 Sheridan was elected to Glasgow City Council to represent the Pollok ward. An MSP from 1999–2007, he was imprisoned after being convicted of perjury in 2011.

Sheridan did this by pioneering a Member's Bill to Abolish Poindings and Warrant Sales, the process by which council tenants in debt could have their possessions seized and sold off to meet their arrears. Sheridan and others had campaigned against such sales in the 1980s and finally saw an opportunity, via the new Scottish Parliament, to end the practice.

This had broad political support, but it took skill and patience to exploit divisions, particularly within the Scottish Labour Party, in order to secure support for the Bill's First Stage in April 2000. Sheridan's speech, however, had an immediate effect. The Scottish Executive withdrew its 'wrecking' amendment minutes before the crucial vote, saying that the mood of the debate (in other words, the prospect of a backbench Labour rebellion) had convinced ministers to allow the Bill to go through to the next stage.

This Bill is part of a long journey. For 300 years, those with power have had access to legal terror. Poindings and warrant sales have been establishment tools of intimidation and fear – tools wielded by the unaccountable and often ruthless sheriff officers to punish the poor for the crime of being poor. Poindings and warrant sales have never been about recovering or resolving debt; they have always been used to humiliate, degrade and frighten the poor. In 1893, the Labour party in Scotland committed itself to abolishing poindings and warrant sales. More than 100 years later, perhaps it is fitting that Scotland's first

Parliament for 300 years has the chance today to seize the opportunity and vote for abolition...

During the past financial year, 23,000 poindings took place and thousands more are taking place in this financial year. I ask members to think of the likes of Mary Ritchie from Govan, who is living on benefits and got herself into arrears of £225 in council tax. She offered the sheriff officers £5 a week in repayment, but they refused it. They demanded a £75 lump-sum payment. Fortunately, Mary got in touch with the Govan Law Centre, which was able to intervene and deliver a repayment schedule of £3 a week from Mary's benefits. What about the countless others who do not know who to get in contact with and who do not

I have often referred to them as Rottweilers in suits.

know where to seek help? They are the ones who are exposed to the ruthlessness of the sheriff officers.

Sheriff officers use the poinding to demand lump-sum payments, forcing those in debt to get themselves into even more debt and then to allow themselves to be exposed at the hands of legal or illegal loan sharks. Colleagues, this is the first Member's Bill and it is the first test of the sovereignty of the parliamentary committees, which have listened to all sides. They have listened to the privileged elites and to the legal establishment: the Law Society of Scotland, the Scottish Law Commission, the Society of Messengers-at-Arms and Sheriff Officers, which represents Scotland's sheriff officers. I have often referred to them as rottweilers in suits, but I must qualify that statement: many rottweilers are often better behaved...

I have little time, so I will appeal to Labour members in particular. In my opinion, the Tories will never represent the poor, so I do not appeal to them to back my bill. The Liberals talk a good game. They talk about how good the committee system is, but when faced with a Bill that has the support of not just one, but three, committees, they are not even prepared to back the motion. I will appeal to Labour members, who may come from a tradition. Did they enter politics as Labour party members to vote against a Bill to abolish poindings and warrant sales?

I ask Labour members to examine their consciences and not to be bullied on this matter. I urge them to support the recommendation of three independent cross-party parliamentary committees, to support what the STUC and their own communities are saying, to take the opportunity today to support Scotland's poor and reject the Executive's wrecking amendment, and to vote for the bill today. (Applause.)

Senator, in everything I said about Iraq I turned out to be right and you turned out to be wrong – and 100,000 have paid with their lives.

George Galloway
1954 –

STATEMENT TO UNITED STATES SENATE HEARING • WASHINGTON DC

17 MAY 2005

George Galloway had always been one of the most articulate, and most controversial, voices in Scottish politics, but when he was re-elected to the Westminster Parliament in 2005 on an anti-war ticket, he stepped up his rhetoric, and became even more controversial. And when *The Daily Telegraph* and *Christian Science Monitor* published documents apparently showing that he had profited from Iraqi oil, the United States Senate moved in for the kill.

A Senate report claimed Galloway and Charles Pasqua, the former French interior minister, had been given potentially lucrative oil allocations as a reward for their support in calling for sanctions against Saddam Hussein's regime to be loosened. Both men denied the claims, and Mr Galloway went to Washington to defend himself with a typically defiant speech.

It is safe to say that the Senators at the hearing were not expecting such a torrent of well-crafted abuse. Even the *Boston Globe* remarked that Galloway was 'known, even in the highly articulate world of British politics, for his memorable turns of phrase'. It was also a good example of oratory uniting people. I remember the feeling in Scotland being 'good on you', and that included people who were hardly admirers of Galloway.

George Galloway was born in 1954 and entered Parliament in 1987 as, initially, the Labour MP for Glasgow Hillhead, and latterly for Glasgow Kelvin. He was expelled from the Labour Party in October 2003 as a result of his public opposition to the Iraq war. Galloway then helped found the left-wing Respect Party and was returned to Parliament on that basis in 2005. He stood in Poplar and Limehouse at the 2010 general election, but was not successful.

SENATOR, I AM NOT NOW, nor have I ever been, an oil trader, and neither has anyone on my behalf. I have never seen a barrel of oil, owned one, bought one, sold one – and neither has anyone on my behalf.

Now I know that standards have slipped in the last few years in Washington, but for a lawyer you are remarkably cavalier with any idea of justice. I am here today but last week you already found me guilty. You traduced my name around the world without ever having asked me a single question, without ever having contacted me, without ever written to me or telephoned me, without any attempt to contact me whatsoever. And you call that justice.

I am here today
but last week you already found me guilty.

Now I want to deal with the pages that relate to me in this dossier and I want to point out areas where there are – let's be charitable and say errors. Then I want to put this in the context where I believe it ought to be. On the very first page of your document about me you assert that I have had 'many meetings' with Saddam Hussein. This is false.

I have had two meetings with Saddam Hussein, once in 1994 and once in August of 2002. By no stretch of the English language can that be described as 'many meetings' with Saddam Hussein.

As a matter of fact, I have met Saddam Hussein exactly the same number of times as Donald Rumsfeld met him. The difference is Donald Rumsfeld met him to sell him guns and to give him maps the better to target those guns. I met him to try and bring about an end to sanctions, suffering and war, and on the second of the two occasions, I met him to try and persuade him to let Dr Hans Blix and the United Nations weapons inspectors back into the country – a rather better use of two meetings with Saddam Hussein than your own Secretary of State for Defence made of his.

I was an opponent of Saddam Hussein when British and American governments and businessmen were selling him guns and gas. I used to demonstrate outside the Iraqi embassy when British and American officials were going in and doing commerce.

I gave my heart and soul
to oppose a policy you promoted.

You will see from the official parliamentary record, Hansard, from the 15th March 1990 onwards, voluminous evidence that I have a rather better record of opposition to Saddam Hussein than you do and than any other member of the British or American governments do.

Now you say in this document, you quote a source, you have the gall to quote a source, without ever having asked me whether the allegation from the source is true, that I am 'the owner of a company which has made substantial profits from trading in Iraqi oil'.

Senator, I do not own any companies, beyond a small company whose entire purpose, whose sole purpose, is to receive the income from my journalistic earnings from my employer, Associated Newspapers, in London. I do not own a company that's been trading in Iraqi oil. And you have no business to carry a quotation, utterly unsubstantiated and false, implying otherwise...

Now, one of the most serious of the mistakes you have made in this set of documents is, to be frank, such a schoolboy howler as to make a fool of the efforts that you have made. You assert on page 19, not once but twice, that the documents that you are referring to cover a different period in time from the documents covered by The Daily Telegraph which were a subject of a libel action won by me in the High Court in England late last year.

You state that The Daily Telegraph article cited documents from 1992 and 1993 whilst you are dealing with documents dating from 2001. Senator, The Daily Telegraph's documents date identically to the documents that you were dealing with in your report here. None of The Daily Telegraph's documents dealt with a period of 1992, 1993. I had never set foot in Iraq until late in 1993 – never in my life. There could possibly be no documents relating to Oil-for-Food matters in 1992, 1993, for the Oil-for-Food scheme did not exist at that time...

> you assert I had
> 'many meetings' with Saddam Hussein.
> This is false.

The existence of forged documents implicating me in commercial activities with the Iraqi regime is a proven fact. It's a proven fact that these forged documents existed and were being circulated amongst right-wing newspapers in Baghdad and around the world in the immediate aftermath of the fall of the Iraqi regime.

Now, Senator, I gave my heart and soul to oppose the policy that you promoted. I gave my political life's blood to try to stop the mass killing of Iraqis by the sanctions on Iraq which killed one million Iraqis, most of them children, most of them died before they even knew that they were Iraqis, but they died for no other reason other than that they were Iraqis with the misfortune to be born at that time. I gave my heart and soul to stop you committing the disaster that you did commit in invading Iraq. And I told the world that your case for the war was a pack of lies...

Senator, in everything I said about Iraq, I turned out to be right and you turned out to be wrong and 100,000 people paid with their lives; 1,600 of them American soldiers sent to their deaths on a pack of lies; 15,000 of them wounded, many of them disabled forever on a pack of lies... Have a look at the real Oil-for-Food scandal. Have a look at the 14 months you were in charge of Baghdad, the first 14 months when $8.8 billion of Iraq's wealth went missing on your watch.

Have a look at Haliburton and other American corporations that stole not only Iraq's money, but the money of the American taxpayer.

Have a look at the oil that you didn't even metre, that you were shipping out of the country and selling, the proceeds of which went who knows where? Have a look at the $800 million you gave to American military commanders to hand out around the country without even counting it or weighing it.

Have a look at the real scandal breaking in the newspapers today, revealed in the earlier testimony in this committee. That the biggest sanctions busters were not me or Russian politicians or French politicians. The real sanctions busters were your own companies with the connivance of your own Government.

Scotland has changed – for good and forever.

Alex Salmond
1954–

SPEECH AT PRESTONFIELD HOUSE HOTEL · EDINBURGH

4 MAY 2007

The Holyrood election of May 2007, in which the Scottish National Party won the most seats for the first time, was an historic event that warranted an historic speech. It had been a long night, with thousands of votes rendered invalid as a result of voter confusion caused by a new ballot paper, and by the time Alex Salmond, the SNP's leader and the man of the moment, made his way from Aberdeenshire to the Scottish capital, the outcome of the election was still not clear.

Nevertheless, Salmond's aides decided to take a gamble and assume the SNP was on course for a narrow victory. The First Minister-to-be took his time as he meandered across the sleek lawn towards a simple lectern that had been erected in front of an expectant media. With a Saltire fluttering behind him and the SNP's election slogan, 'It's Time', static beneath his microphone, Salmond began to speak. 'Talking like a First Minister,' observed one journalist present, 'sounding like a president.'[37]

Alexander Elliot Anderson Salmond was born in Linlithgow on Hogmanay 1954. After St Andrews University he worked for the Royal Bank of Scotland before entering the House of Commons in 1987. He was elected leader of the SNP in 1990 and served until 2000, returning four years later. Salmond was first elected First Minister of a minority Scottish Government in 2007 and re-elected on gaining an overall majority at the 2011 Holyrood election.

AFTER WHAT WAS A momentous night in Scottish politics, and with all votes still not counted, it is I hope appropriate that I say a few words about where Scotland now stands.

First, I recognise that this election has profoundly unsettled Scotland and every Scot who believes in a transparent and open democracy. The events of last night will have offended every democrat in this country and those watching from around the world.

In the event that the Scottish people have indeed chosen the SNP as a party of Government – and that prospect looks ever more likely – let me therefore make a first pledge as a prospective First Minister.

My first act will be to announce an independent judicial inquiry into the debacle of the 2007 Scottish Parliamentary elections.

Not an inquiry within the corridors of power and not even an inquiry such as that proposed today by the Electoral Commission but rather a vigorous and robustly independent judicial inquiry.

> *We will lead with verve and imagination*
> *but always mindful that we serve the people*
> *— all the people — of this proud and ancient nation.*

That inquiry will have the fullest powers of recovery of evidence and the most searching remit. It will be charged with laying bare the outrage of over 100,000 Scots being denied their democratic voice. It will have access to every shred of evidence and every technical assistance to understand precisely what caused the events of last night.

The inquiry is therefore charged with no less a task than restoring the confidence of the people of Scotland in their democratic process. A task that important must be carried out by an inquiry free of even the slightest hint of Government involvement. Scotland will demand no less. And, if charged with the responsibility of leadership, I will deliver no less.

Secondly, against the uncertain backdrop of these elections, let me try to offer clarity. Scotland has changed – for good and forever. There may be Labour Governments and Labour First Ministers in the decades to come but never again will we see the Labour Party assume that it has a divine right to rule. Scotland has chosen a new path – one which echoes the hopes and aspirations of a new culture of politics. Last night was a reminder that politicians exist to serve and not just to survive.

> *There is an immense task*
> *ahead of a new Government but it is one which*
> *should inspire and not deter.*

Thirdly, I am now proud to be in a position to announce that, regardless of the electoral arithmetic to follow, the SNP has won the highest number of votes of any party in the election.

That is a historic moment and let me give one more commitment on behalf of my party. If the SNP is given the chance to lead, we will do so in the national interest and not for party advantage. We will lead with humility but also with passion. We will lead with verve and imagination but always mindful that we serve the people – all the people – of this proud and ancient nation.

There is an immense task ahead of a new Government but it is one which should inspire and not deter.

The Scottish writer Alasdair Gray put it well when he wrote – 'Work as though you lived in the early days of a better nation'.

My commitment to Scotland is this – we will work, and these are the early days of a better nation.

Endnotes

Introduction

1 Richard Aldous, *Great Irish Speeches*, Quercus, London, 2007.

2 'May the Devil cause you severe pains in your abdomen, false thief: dare you say the Mass in my ear?'

John Inglis

3 AD Smith, ed, *The Trial of Madeleine Smith*, William Hodge, Edinburgh, 1921, 285.

4 James Crabb Watt, *John Inglis: A Memoir*, William Green, Edinburgh, 1893, 89.

Henry George

5 Henry George, *Progress and Poverty*, Cambridge University Press, Cambridge, 2009, 11.

6 Philip Snowden, *An Autobiography*, Ivor Nicholson & Watson, London, 1934, 49.

Keir Hardie

7 Emrys Hughes, *Keir Hardie*, Allen & Unwin, London, 1956, 61.

David Kirkwood

8 David Kirkwood, *My Life of Revolt*, Harrap, London, 1935, 94–97.

9 *The Times* 22/4/1955.

JM Barrie

10 Lisa Chaney, *Hide and Seek with Angels: A Life of JM Barrie*, Hutchinson, London, 2005, 374.

Lord Birkenhead

11 doi:10.1093/ref:odnb/36137.

Ramsay MacDonald

12 David Marquand, *Ramsay MacDonald*, Jonathan Cape, London, 1977, 303.

Duchess of Atholl

13 SJ Hetherington, *Katharine Atholl: Against the Tide*, Aberdeen University Press, Aberdeen, 1989, 101.

HH Asquith

14 Roy Jenkins, *Asquith*, Collins, London, 1964, 517.

15 This quote is from 'The Sundial' by Thomas Love Peacock.

Edward Rosslyn Mitchell

16 The Battle of Naseby was a key battle in the English Civil War, at which King Charles I's army was defeated by Oliver Cromwell's Parliamentarian New Model army on 14 June 1645.

Edwin Scrymgeour

17 Hansard, vol. 224, c156, 29/10/1930.

Sir Compton Mackenzie

18 Andro Linklater, *Compton Mackenzie: A Life*, Chatto & Windus, London, 1987, 238–39.

John Buchan

19 Andrew Lownie, *John Buchan: The Presbyterian Cavalier*, Pimlico, London, 2002, 210.

20 Henry Dundas, 1st Viscount Melville and Baron Dunira (1742–1811), was a lawyer and politician who exercised considerable influence over the governance of Scotland in the late 18th century.

21 Quoted in Tait's Edinburgh magazine, volume 21, from a letter to John Wilson Croker.

Florence Horsbrugh

22 This is a reference to John Knox's 1558 polemic 'The First Blast of the Trumpet Against the Monstrous Regimen of Women'.

George Buchanan

23 John Paton, *Left Turn: The Autobiography*, Secker & Warburg, London, 1936, 225.

Winston Churchill

24 Martin Gilbert, *Winston S Churchill: Finest Hour*, Heinemann, London, 1983, 990.

Robert McIntyre

25 Harold Nicolson, *Diaries and Letters 1939–45*, Collins, London, 1967, 449.

John Reith

26 Ian McIntyre, *The Expense of Glory: A life of John Reith*, HarperCollins, London, 1993, 309.

Robert Boothby

27 Lord Boothby, *My Yesterday, Your Tomorrow*, Hutchison, London, 1962, 47.

Wendy Wood

28 Wendy Wood, *Yours Sincerely for Scotland*, Barker, London, 1970, 198.

29 doi:10.1993/ref:odnb/40380.

Miss Jean Brodie

30 Jay Presson Allen, *The Prime of Miss Jean Brodie: A Drama in Three Acts*, Samuel French, London, 2006.

Mick McGahey

31 71st Report of the Scottish Trades Union Congress, 398–409.

David Steel

32 Stuart Mole, *The Decade of Realignment: The Leadersip Speeches of David Steel 1976–1986*, Hebden Royd, Hebden Bridge, 1986, 8.

Margaret Thatcher

33 Margaret Thatcher, *The Path to Power*, HarperCollins, London, 1995, 555.

34 Harry Reid, *Outside Verdict: An Old Kirk in a New Scotland*, St Andrew Press, Edinburgh, 2001, 164.

Renton

35 John Hodge & Irvine Welsh, *Trainspotting: A Screenplay*, Faber & Faber, London, 1996.

John Smith

36 Brian Brivati, ed, *Guiding Light: The Collected Speeches of John Smith*, Politico's, London, 2000, 253.

Alex Salmond

37 *Scottish Daily Mail* 5/5/2007.

The BBC in Scotland: The First 50 Years
David Pat Walker
ISBN 978 1908373 00 7 HBK £20

The key figure in the story of British broadcasting was a Scot, John Reith, who took great personal interest in the development of the British Broadcasting Company (later Corporation) in Scotland. But who were these early Scottish broadcasters? What were their challenges? What did they achieve? How did the service grow over its first 50 years?

David Pat Walker offers an insider's look at the events that shaped the nation's broadcaster. From the early, frantic radio broadcasts of the 1920s to coded war broadcasts and the promotion of Scottish drama, the BBC's first 50 years served to define an institution whose influence continues to the present day.

A Word for Scotland
Jack Campbell
ISBN 978 0946487 48 6 PBK £12.99

The inside story of a newspaper and a nation. Five tumultuous decades as they happened.

A Word for Scotland was Lord Beaverbrook's hope when he founded the *Scottish Daily Express*. That word for Scotland quickly became, and was for many years, the national paper of Scotland.

Jack joined the infant newspaper at the age of 15 as a copy boy and went on to become the managing editor. He remembers the early days of news gathering on a shoestring, the circulation wars, all the scoops and dramas and tragedies through nearly half a century of the most exciting, innovative and competitive years of the press in Scotland.

This book is a fascinating reminder of Scottish journalism in its heyday. It will be read avidly by those journalists who take pride in their profession – and should be compulsory reading for those that don't.
JACK WEBSTER

Homage to Caledonia

Daniel Gray

ISBN 978 1906817 16 9 PBK £9.99

If I don't go and fight fascism, I'll just have to wait and fight it here.
JOHN 'PATSY' McEWAN, *Dundee*

What drove so many ordinary Scots to volunteer for a foreign war?

Their stories are simply and honestly told, often in their own words: the soldiers who made their own way to Spain over the Pyrenees when the UK government banned anyone from going to support either side; the nurses and ambulance personnel who discovered for themselves the horrors of modern warfare that struck down women and children as well as their men. Yet for every tale of distress and loss, there is a tale of a drunken Scottish volunteer urinating in his general's boots, the dark comedy of learning to shoot with sticks as rifles were so scarce, or lying about their age to get into the training camps.

Daniel Gray has written a deeply human history, moving and thought-provoking, not only of those 549 people, but of two nations – Scotland and Spain – battling with an evil that would soon darken the whole of Europe.
THE HERALD

The Prisoner of St Kilda: The True Story of the Unfortunate Lady Grange

Margaret Macaulay

ISBN 978 1906817 65 7 PBK £8.99

One shotgun wedding.

Two kings.

Thirteen years incarcerated.

Married to a Scottish law lord, Lady Grange threatened to expose her husband's secret connections to the Jacobites in an attempt to force him to leave his London mistress. But the stakes were higher than she could ever have imagined. Her husband's powerful co-conspirators exacted a ruthless revenge. She was carried off to the Western Isles, doomed to 13 bitter years of captivity. Death was her only release.

The Prisoner of St Kilda looks beyond the legends to tell for the first time the true story of an extraordinary woman.

It's a stunning story and Margaret Macaulay has done it full justice.
THE HERALD

A story of political intrigue, betrayal and personal tragedy.
THE SUNDAY POST

Blind Ossian's Fingal

James Macpherson

ISBN 978 1906817 55 8 HBK £15.00

To the accompaniment of the harp, Ossian enchanted his third-century listeners with tales of savage battles, magnanimous victories, graceful defeats, doomed romances and bloody feuds.

The rediscovered Ossianic epics inspired the Romantic movement in Europe, but caused a political storm in Britain and up to recently have been denounced as one of the greatest literary hoaxes of all time.

When James Macpherson published his translations of the poetry of Ossian, a third-century Highland bard, they were an instant success. However, the plaudits soon gave way to controversy. Were the poems part of a great Gaelic oral tradition, or the work of Macpherson's imagination?

They contain the purest and most animating principles and examples of true honour, courage and discipline, and all the heroic virtues that can possibly exist.

NAPOLEON

Poems, Chiefly in the Scottish Dialect: The Luath Kilmarnock Edition

Robert Burns

With contributions from John Cairney and Clarke McGinn, illustrated by Bob Dewar

ISBN 978 1906307 67 7 HBK £15

Poems, Chiefly in the Scottish Dialect, was the first collection of poetry produced by Robert Burns. Published in Kilmarnock in July 1786, it contains some of his best known poems including 'The Cotter's Saturday Night', 'To a Mouse', 'The Twa Dogs' and 'To a Mountain Daisy'. *The Luath Kilmarnock Edition* brings this classic of Scottish literature back into print, after being unavailable for many years.

New material includes an introduction by the 'Man Who Played Burns' – author, actor and Burns expert John Cairney – exploring Burns' life and work, especially the origins of the *Kilmarnock Edition*. Looking to the future of Burns in Scotland and the rest of the world, Clark McGinn, world-renowned Burns Supper speaker, provides an afterword that speaks to Burns' continuing legacy. This edition is illustrated throughout by original line drawings by top political satirist Bob Dewar.

Arts of Resistance: Poets, Portraits and Landscapes of Modern Scotland

Alan Riach and Alexander Moffat, with contributions by Linda MacDonald-Lewis
ISBN 978 1906817 18 3 PBK £16.99

Arts:

1 Any imaginative or creative narrative, or non-scientific branch of knowledge eg. literature, history, fine art, music

2 ingenious abilities or schemes

Resistance:

1 Standing firm, refusing to submit

2 A covert organisation fighting for national liberty in a country under enemy occupation

The role of art in the modern world is to challenge and provoke, to resist stagnation and to question complacency. All art, whether poetry, painting or prose, represents and interprets the world. Its purpose is to bring new perspectives to what life can be.
ALEXANDER MOFFAT and ALAN RIACH

... an inspiration, a revelation and education as to the extraordinary richness and organic cohesion of 20th-century Scottish culture, full of intellectual adventure... a landmark book.
TIMES LITERARY SUPPLEMENT

A Gray Play Book

Alasdair Gray
ISBN 978 1906307 91 2 PBK £25.00

A Gray Play Book is an anthology of long and short plays for stage, radio and television, acted between 1956 and 2009. It also includes an unperformed opera libretto, excerpts from the *Lanark* storyboard and the full film script of the novel *Poor Things* by Alasdair Gray.

Gray wrote plays before becoming known as a novelist, and has recently had new works staged. Over 50 years of them are collected here with prefaces, making this a Scots playwright's autobiography.

Over 50 years' worth of Alasdair Gray's dramatic works appear in the hugely enjoyable A Gray Play Book... Fans of Gray's self-termed 'comic fantasies' will also enjoy the candid prefaces that explain how each play was written and produced.
SCOTTISH REVIEW OF BOOKS

Details of these and other books published by Luath Press can be found at:

www.luath.co.uk

Luath Press Limited

committed to publishing well written books worth reading

LUATH PRESS takes its name from Robert Burns, whose little collie Luath (*Gael.,* swift or nimble) tripped up Jean Armour at a wedding and gave him the chance to speak to the woman who was to be his wife and the abiding love of his life. Burns called one of 'The Twa Dogs' Luath after Cuchullin's hunting dog in Ossian's *Fingal*. Luath Press was established in 1981 in the heart of Burns country, and now resides a few steps up the road from Burns' first lodgings on Edinburgh's Royal Mile.
Luath offers you distinctive writing with a hint of unexpected pleasures.

Most bookshops in the UK, the US, Canada, Australia, New Zealand and parts of Europe either carry our books in stock or can order them for you. To order direct from us, please send a £sterling cheque, postal order, international money order or your credit card details (number, address of cardholder and expiry date) to us at the address below. Please add post and packing as follows: UK – £1.00 per delivery address; overseas surface mail – £2.50 per delivery address; overseas airmail – £3.50 for the first book to each delivery address, plus £1.00 for each additional book by airmail to the same address. If your order is a gift, we will happily enclose your card or message at no extra charge.

ILLUSTRATION: IAN KELLAS

Luath Press Limited
543/2 Castlehill
The Royal Mile
Edinburgh EH1 2ND
Scotland

Telephone: 0131 225 4326 (24 hours)
Fax: 0131 225 4324
email: sales@luath.co.uk
Website: www.luath.co.uk